Maturing in Sonship through Suffering

McDougal & Associates
Servants of Christ and Stewards of the
Mysteries of God

I0167902

Maturing in Sonship through Suffering

By

Sheila Kay

MATURING IN SONSHIP THROUGH SUFFERING
Copyright © 2016 by Sheila M. Kay
ALL RIGHTS RESERVED UNDER U.S., LATIN AMERI-
CAN AND INTERNATIONAL COPYRIGHTS
No part of this book may be reproduced or transmitted in any
form or by any means—electronic or mechanical, including pho-
tocopying, recording, or by any information storage and retrieval
system—without written permission from the author except as
provided by the copyright laws of the United States of America.
Unauthorized reproduction is a violation of international law.

Unless otherwise noted, all scripture quotations are from the 21st
Century King James Version of the Bible, © 1994 by Deuel En-
terprises, Inc. References marked JUB are from the Jubilee Bible,
© 2000, 2001, 2010 by LIFE SENTENCE Publishing. References
marked LEB are from the Lexham English Bible, © 2012 by Lo-
gos Bible Software. References marked NKJV are from the *Holy
Bible, New King James Version,* copyright © 1979, 1980, 1982,
1990 by Thomas Nelson, Inc., Nashville, Tennessee.

Cover design by Scotty Roberts
www.scottalanroberts.com

Published by:

McDougal & Associates
18896 Greenwell Springs Road
Greenwell Springs, LA 70739
www.thepublishedword.com

ISBN 978-1-940461-53-3

Printed on demand in the U.S., the U.K. and Australia
For worldwide distribution

Dedication

To my wonderful children—Jeffrey, Jeneene, Catherine and Jodie—and my two sons-in-law—Mike K. and Mike B. Thank you for your prayers and for supporting me as I work diligently to fulfill the call of God on my life. Thank you for standing by my side, for coming to my meetings, and for spending time with me at camp. I love each of you very much, and I am blessed by your lives.

To my four grandchildren—John, Joe, Jessica and Tommy—and great-grandchild Danielle Elizabeth, who, as children, all looked at me strangely as I told you about my spiritual revelations. My prayer is that you realize the beauty of walking in the cool of the day with the Lord and that He becomes your Best Friend throughout life, as He has been for me. I love you all so much.

Acknowledgments

My love and eternal gratitude go to my Lord and Savior Jesus Christ and to the Comforter who lives within me. To God, who talked to me when I was seven years old, as flickering sunlight coming through the foliage of trees in the forest.

When I look back over my life, I realize that God was with me all the time, bringing me through every bad situation. He then used each traumatic event that occurred in my life to help others. But it took purging and years and years of molding to bring me to a mature sonship.

The Word of God taught me to be obedient, that when He speaks we are to react or respond immediately, and we are to be yielded vessels.

He taught me to forgive those who had violated me, and to pray for those whom I thought I hated.

My first ministry was named Restoring the Broken Vessel, and I was that broken vessel which God restored. He is continuously maturing me in sonship, while allowing me to be a conduit He can use here on this earth.

Special

†✝†

Periodically throughout the book you will see this image, and when you do, you will know what it means:

The center cross represents Jesus, our Savior.

The cross to the left represents the sinner who believed in Jesus and was forgiven. He will spend eternity with Christ in an atmosphere of love and beauty.

The cross to the right represents the thief who rejected Jesus. He will spend eternity separated from Christ and all that is good and loving. We have all been given a choice. Choose you today whom you will serve.

These crosses represent a crossroads in our life, and we all are given an opportunity to make a critical choice. Why not live for Him because He died for you?

Pages

†††

Periodically, throughout the book, you will also see this symbol, and when you do, you will know what it means:

My desire, in relating to you, the reader, the events that have transpired in my life, is to inspire you to love and worship the Creator, who alone is worthy of praise. These "How to Worship" sections are meant to encourage you to develop your own intimate relationship with Him.

Man shall not live by bread alone, but by every Word that proceeds out of the mouth of God.

Matthew 4:4, JUB

Contents

Who Is Shelia Kay?..13

Preface..15

Introduction...17

1. Angels on Assignment.............................23

2. God Ordained Gifts.................................37

3. The Eyes Are the Window of the Soul........51

4. An Unction Saves a Life 65

5. A New Name Written Down in Glory 73

6. A Prophetic Vision 83

7. Forgiveness Saved My Life 91

8. One Step at a Time 105

9. A Prophetic Dream.................................113

10. "Sit at Her Feet" 123

11. "Sit Next to Claire on the Plane" 133

12. Jail and Street Ministry 139

13. "In the Body or Out," I Do Not Know.......143

14. "Choose You This Day Whom Ye will Serve". 149

15. "I Am the Lord that Healeth Thee" 165

16. A Christmas Gift from God 173

17. Leading More Men and Woman to Christ 179

18. My Love Child 199

19. Releasing Your Yesterdays 213

20. The Father Weeps 221

21. Rough Beginnings 227

22. Favor in My Father's Eyes............................235

23. Private Time with God 243

24. Continually Thanking God 249

25. In Conclusion 255

Prayers to the Father 258

About the Author...262

Author Contact Page 266

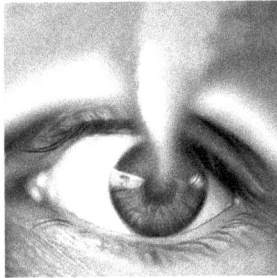

Who Is Sheila Kay?

You may not know me, so let me tell you a little bit about myself, who I AM:

- I am in this world but not of it!
- I am a spirit being in a human body, just as Jesus was when He came to this earth!
- I love to worship Him!
- I am a firm believer in Jesus Christ!
- I am a child of the King!
- I am saved and water baptized!
- I am sanctified!
- I am Holy Ghost filled!
- My body has been healed!
- I have a new name written down in Glory!

- I speak a new language, and I am living for the Lord!
- I am a vessel, a conduit, a human body through which my Father works in this world!
- His Holy Spirit lives within me!
- No matter what I've done or what I have been through, it has molded me, and I have been forgiven!
- I am a new creation in Christ Jesus, and I am now here to serve!
- I have surrendered this vessel to Him and today I know my purpose, and I am born again!

Sheila

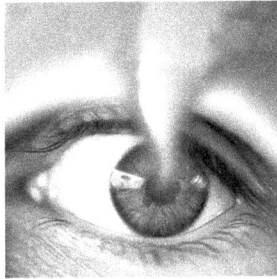

Preface

When the right time comes concerning the next great outpouring of the Holy Spirit and all the mighty works that will follow such a marvelous event, it will be necessary (and the duty of each one of us) to record his or her authentic information to contribute to the past history of the Church and also as the Church makes new history. The greater part of what I have written on the following pages is from firsthand information and personal revelation from God Almighty Himself.

My eyes have seen His mighty works, but I am convinced that all of this is just leading up to a great revival that is about to take place. I humbly acknowledge that I am yet a work in progress, while giving all praise, honor and glory to the Triune God I serve, for He saved me from a life of shame, covering all my sins with His precious blood.

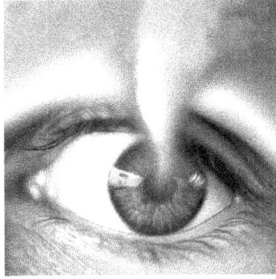

Introduction

Sonship is a term commonly used among Christians to describe our rights and privileges as sons of God, and these rights are vast. However, there is also a vast difference between infant sons, childish sons and grown, or mature, sons. Those who are no longer children in their faith, but have matured into adulthood can do so much more. So much more is entrusted to them, and so much more is expected of them.

In olden times, a Jewish man could not become a priest until he turned thirty. This was Jesus' age when He stepped out into His ministry and was declared to be God's *"beloved Son"*:

You are My beloved Son; in You I am well pleased. Luke 3:32, NKJV

In the same way, David was not anointed king over Israel until he was thirty (see 2 Samuel 5:4). Mature sons are no longer babes but full-grown in both the physical and the spiritual. They are ready for a higher calling.

When we choose to pursue a higher calling in God, we should be aware that mature and trusted sons must follow spiritual protocols or principles and a biblical course of action. Those who truly hunger and thirst for the meat of the spiritual life will need to know and fulfill such protocols and will need to know what is biblically required of them.

Mature sons must never be men-pleasers. Rather, they are called to be God-pleasers. They must not be self-seeking, and they must never act out of hurt or rejection, nor pursue their own agendas. They must never harbor grudges or hurts, no matter how justified these may seem. Furthermore, mature sons must learn to bear the burdens of their younger brothers and sisters.

True sons of God are led by the Holy Spirit:

For as many as are led by the Spirit of God, these are sons of God. Romans 8:14, NKJV

True sons must be willing to be sacrificed:

He who did not withhold his own Son, but gave him up for all of us, will he not with him also give us everything else? Romans 8:32, NRSV

Sonship and heirship are related:

So that you are no longer a slave [servant] but a son, and if a son, also an heir through God.
Galatians 4:7, LEB

But what can a childish son do with an inheritance?

A full grown spiritual son no longer needs the Hebrew Law and elementary instruction and guidance, but rather, he operates on faith that has progressively grown through dedication to the Word of God. And there is another element that leads to maturity, one that we often don't want to recognize or contemplate.

With my own eyes, I have seen God's mighty works, but I have noticed that He uses tests of all kinds to prepare those whom He has chosen, to see what level of obedience they possess and how well they listen to His commands—whether they put them on the back burner, ignore them, or respond immediately.

It makes a difference. Our God has made it quite clear that if He cannot trust us, He cannot use us. It is with obedience that promotion comes. In the days ahead, each of us must heed His call and remain watchful and diligent, as we dedicate our love, faithfulness and trust to the Father, Son and Holy Spirit, the great Three in One.

Through faith, an unwavering belief in the Word of Almighty God, we grow, mature, and move from glory, to glory, to glory. But it is through numerous trials that we learn that He is our Anchor in every storm and learn to cry out to our ever-present and loving God and rely only on Him. In return for His love, we must learn to love and worship Him as He deserves. Once this level of surrender is reached, we become the mature sons God has so longed for.

While we could never record every event or every step that has led to our maturity, on the following pages I hope to give you an insight into the miraculous workings and revelations that have taken place with me, my family, my friends, and others, as God bridged us together for advancing from glory to glory, being led by the Holy Spirit into a more mature sonship.

I must warn you that my story is not told in any logical sequence. I wrote the book as the Lord brought each incident to my remembrance. Join me now on a journey toward *Maturing in Sonship through Suffering.*

Sheila Kay
Waldorf, Maryland

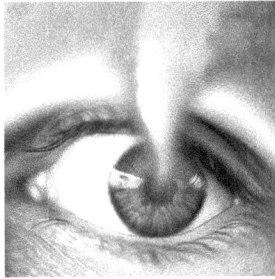

~ ONE~

Angels on Assignment

*Are they not all ministering spirits, sent forth to min-
ister for those who shall be heirs of salvation?*

Hebrews 1:14

It was a beautiful December day in historic
Fredericksburg, Virginia. The sun was beginning
to go down toward the west, for it was about 4
p.m., and I was leaving a four-day Randy Clark
Healing/Training Seminar. The deer were beginning to feed at dusk along the hilly rural roads
through the King George countryside. Hopefully it would still be daylight when I arrived home
in lower southern Maryland, a forty-five-minute
drive on a good day.

I had traveled only about half a mile or so on the very busy highway. Christmas shoppers were out, and traffic was extremely heavy. When the traffic signal turned green, I began to maneuver toward the right, to avoid the backup from those in the extended left-turn lane that led into a shopping center.

My thoughts were on my husband Bill and what I would prepare for our dinner. He was retired and often chose to prepare our meals himself, but he had been having some health issues recently, and I hadn't been sure just when I would be home. So dinner was up to me, and I wasn't sure whether I would need to stop by the grocery store or just wait until I got closer to home. Suddenly a clear voice came within me. It was a voice I had heard many times before. It said, "Turn into the parking lot at this restaurant!"

"But, Lord, I'm not hungry," was my first thought. There was no reply.

I knew what I had heard, so I was obedient and pulled into the crowded parking lot of a national chain restaurant.

As I exited my car and approached the front door of the restaurant, there was a clean-cut young man sitting on a bench to the left of the entrance. I remember thinking he must have come from the conference, for he had a Christian look about him. I smiled as I passed, and he returned the smile.

The restaurant greeter led me to a two-seater booth and held out a menu. "No thanks," I said, "I'll just have a small house salad with Italian dressing and an unsweetened iced tea, please," and she went off to get my order.

There was a large Christmas shopping crowd in the restaurant, and my eyes began to scan the festive decorations and suddenly fell upon a table that was kitty-cornered to my small booth. There was a small child in a high chair, a girl. She was wearing a beautiful red velvet dress with white fur on the cuffs of the sleeves and around the hem. Her grandma was breaking up crackers on the table for her. Looking at the whole family—mom, dad, grandma, grandpa, and grandchild—I knew they had just come from Olin Mills Studio, from having Christmas photos taken, probably for a Christmas card.

The waiter returned and placed my salad and tea on the table in front of me. I began to sip on the tea, thinking how that family looked like a Norman

Rockwell painting. That thought soon left when suddenly the Holy Spirit spoke to me, "Go over to that table and tell them to take the crackers off the tabletop because those red tiles have lead paint on them."

I paused a moment. "Lord is that You? Or is this just me?"

Then, again, I heard the same words: "Go over to that table and tell them to take the crackers off the tabletop because the red tiles have lead paint on them."

A hand nudged me to get up, and I could feel another hand gently pushing me in my back ribs. It was telling me to get up—now.

Taking my napkin from my lap, I laid it on the table and took the four steps it would require to get to the other table. I reached out softly and touched the grandmother on her right shoulder and said, "Excuse me. I know you're going to think I'm crazy, but God just spoke to me and asked me to tell you to take the crackers off the table. Those tiles have lead paint on them."

Immediately she began sweeping up the crackers from the tabletop into the palm of her hand, never making eye contact with me. Then she opened up a paper napkin and spread it neatly before the child and began breaking fresh pieces of saltine crackers onto it, to keep her beautiful granddaughter entertained as they waited for their meals to come.

No one at the table spoke, and I quickly returned to my small booth and motioned for the waiter to bring my check. My mood was of total embarrassment. I just wanted to get out of there as fast as I could.

After signing the credit card slip for my meal, I got up to leave. Then, when I was halfway past the other table, God stopped me. I turned and spoke directly to the father of the child. "I'm sorry if I, in any way, disturbed your lunch today," I said.

The little girl's father was very distinguished looking, and I was almost certain it was his mother who was feeding the eighteen-month-old. He spoke now in a slow southern accent, introducing himself as the pastor of one of the largest Baptist churches in the area. He went on to say, "I want to thank you for your obedience and boldness in giving me that word of knowledge."

I smiled a thank-you, as he continued. "That message was not for my mother but for me. I have been questioning whether God even connects with His children anymore."

Again I smiled, nodded and said, "Thank you for that, Reverend," and then turned and walked away.

Wow! Wow, God! Look at You!

My excitement level was through the roof. I could not believe God had sent me to Fredericksburg, Virginia to give a word of knowledge to the pastor of one of the largest churches in the historic part of town. I knew at that moment I had been used by God to deliver a message for the purpose of showing four Christian adults that God is alive and well. He was concerned with how they felt about Him, and He was saying to them, "Return to your first love."

God wanted to use that pastor and He wanted him to know and believe that the gifts of the Spirit are still in operation today. In this way, revival could come to a beautiful inner-city Baptist church.

That experience not only woke something up in that pastor; it also woke something up in me. Never had I experienced such a thing, and the excitement of it had placed a smile on my face and a spring in my step.

As I thought back on the experience, I realized that I hadn't really wanted to follow the prompting of the Spirit. It was embarrassing. I still didn't know the whys and wherefores of it, but I knew that God had just used me in a mighty way, and I was praising Him for it.

As I exited the restaurant that day, I noticed the same young man still seated on that bench. I smiled at him again, and he again returned the smile. No words were spoken.

After starting my car, I adjusted the level of the praise and worship music. The presence of the Holy Spirit was so strong on me and the car was so filled with it that, in my joy, I almost wanted to weep.

Suddenly I could feel someone staring at me. In my head I was saying, "Lord, don't let anyone ask me for a ride today. This is a strange town, and I don't know my way around."

I turned and, much to my surprise, there stood the young man from the bench. "Lord," I prayed, "please don't let him need a ride. I don't know him, and I certainly don't know this town. Please! Please! Please!"

Slowly I pushed the button to lower the window and asked, "May I help you?"

His response was, "I feel led to pray for you!"

I couldn't help but think that was a rather unusual choice of words: "I feel led to pray."

Again my thought was that this young man must have been at the same Spirit-filled conference I had attended earlier in the day, for there was something special about him. The anointing at the conference had been awesome, with miracles, signs and wonders in evidence. We had all been "flying high" with the presence and glory of God.

As I thought now on this young man's statement, "I feel led ... ," I found his choice of words unusual. Most people would have said, "May I pray for you?" This sparked my interest I questioned in my mind where this had come from. Could this be an angel?

I smiled and answered him, "Great! But first let me tell you what just happened inside the restaurant." I was still very elated with the experience and wanted to share it with someone who would understand, so that I could give glory to God. A fellow Spirit-filled Christian would understand—even if he happened to be a total stranger.

As I related the experience now, I was amazed at the lack of excitement from the young man. It was not just a lack of excitement; there was no reaction at all.

Then, once again, he said, "I feel led to pray for you."

I lowered my window all the way down and rested my arm in the opening, and the young man immediately placed his hand on my forearm, near the elbow. Then, from out of nowhere, there suddenly appeared another man next to him, and he also placed his hand on my arm, but more toward the wrist area.

The first man was fair skinned and had sandy colored hair. The second man was taller, more of an olive skin tone, and his hair was dark.

There was no further conversation. No more words were spoken after, "I feel led to pray for you," and there was also no eye contact. This was strange.

Both men began to pray, and I listened intently to every word they said. As I did, tears began seeping from my eyes.

It was a long prayer, a beautiful prayer, as I remember it. Then it was over, and the two men turned and walked away together and entered the restaurant. I knew immediately that if I were to enter the restaurant I would never find those two men. In my spirit, I sensed that I had just been prayed over by real angels.

Inside the restaurant earlier, I had been tested on listening to God, following His instructions, on understanding and on obedience. Now this.

As I exited from the parking lot, continuing my journey home, I began to weep over the entire experience. What had happened in the restaurant with the word of knowledge and then outside with the angels praying over me, was simply overwhelming.

It seemed important, so I tried to remember the specific words they had prayed over me, but I could not remember even one. And they were gone. The Spirit showed me that this word had been sealed up within me until the time He would use me in a greater way. What had been placed within me was for a later date and time.

From then on, whenever I think of what He placed in me, I have realized it was because of my faith in Him and my obedience and faithfulness. This made me want to respond immediately the next time He spoke to me and the time after that, and to every call He sent my way. The experience had built my faith even stronger.

For anyone questioning the part about the angels, angels were active throughout the New Testament record, as special messengers of God. The writer of Hebrews stated:

Are they not all ministering spirits, sent forth to minister for those who shall be heirs of salvation?
Hebrews 1:14

What appeared to be two men had prayed over me in a restaurant parking lot, but they had really been angels, angels on assignment. This was God's glorious intervention in my life, as He transformed my spirit and my soul.

That first angel had been seated at the door awaiting his assignment. I tend to believe that if I had not responded with obedience to the three commands I was given: 1) Turn into the restaurant parking lot, 2) Go over to that table, and 3) Apologize before you leave, the angel would not have acted. His assignment depended on my obedience.

Be not forgetful to entertain strangers: for thereby some have entertained angels unawares.
Hebrews 11:2

I was convinced that even more exciting days lay ahead. I was *Maturing in Sonship through Suffering.*

☩

Here are a few references concerning the appearance of angels to men throughout Bible history.

IN THE OLD TESTAMENT

Hagar	Genesis 16:7-11 and 21:17
Abraham	Genesis 18:2, 22:11 and 15
Lot and the Sodomites	Genesis 9:1-22
Jacob	Genesis 28:12, 31:11 and 32:1
Moses	Exodus 3:2
Balaam	Numbers 22:22-35
Joshua	Exodus 23:20-23
Israel	Judges 2:1-5
Gideon	Judges 6:1-22
Manoah's wife	Judges 13:3-5 and 9:21
David	2 Samuel 24, and 1 Chronicles 21
Elijah	1 Kings 19:5-7 and 2 Kings 6:6-17
The Assyrians	2 Kings 19:35 and Isaiah37:36
The Hebrew children	Daniel 3:25-28, 6:22, 8:16 and 9:21

IN THE NEW TESTAMENT

New Testament appearances of angels include the following:

To Zechariah	(7 times)
To Joseph	(3 times)
To Mary	
To Zacharias	
To the Shepherds	
To Jesus	
To the women	
To the disciples	
To Peter and John	
To Philip	
To Cornelius	
To Peter	
To Paul	
To John	
To the Body of Christ	1 Corinthians 12:13-30

✝ ✝ ✝

How to Worship

Read 1 Chronicles 16:9

Sing psalms unto Him.

Sing about His wondrous

works.

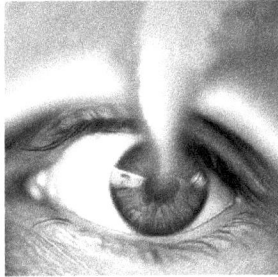

~ TWO ~

God-Ordained Gifts

And God has appointed these in the church: first apostles, second prophets, third teachers, after that miracles, then gifts of healings, helps, administrations, varieties of tongues.

1 Corinthians 12:28, NKJV

Because I was an early riser, I often took those first hours of the day as private personal time to spend with the Lord. Bill was retired and enjoyed sleeping in, and that gave me the first hours of every day to have quality time with my first love—Jesus.

In those hours of private time with the Lord, I not only prayed and worshiped and soaked in His glorious presence; I also read His Word, studying and cross-referencing it to gain more understanding. There could be no more wonderful way to begin every day!

It was September 2, 2001, and at 6 a.m. I was reading and studying the book of Genesis, using several different Bibles and commentaries, as I cross-referenced various topics and words. Suddenly I heard what I believed to be the audible voice of God. It came so very clear — soft, yet perfect. "You are to teach," said the Lord.

How wonderful was that? God, the Creator of Heaven and Earth, God, my Creator, had taken time out of His busy schedule to talk to me.

Bill had been a deacon in the Southern Baptist Church in nearby St. Charles for more than twenty years, and I was afraid that if I told him I had heard the audible voice of God, he would think I was losing it. So I decided not to mention it to him until later. I was very excited about this new gift God had given me and didn't want to lose that feeling of excitement.

That Saturday morning we hooked up the home-made pig cooker we had purchased in North Carolina, loaded up our other catering gear and headed for the riverside home of the

Tippett family. This beautiful family let our church use their waterfront property, with its boats and swimming pool, every year for our annual church picnic. Since Bill and I had a part-time catering business, we almost always helped with the food for the events.

As we were nearing the picnic location, I was enjoying the wonderful end of summer and the beginning of fall weather, just taking in the rich, full greenery of the landscape. Suddenly, God spoke to me again, just as He had before. Again it was audible. "You are to teach," He said.

I quickly looked over at Bill, to see if he had heard anything. He hadn't. Within myself I answered God, "Lord, if You want me to teach, You must show me where and how to start."

Within a few minutes we were at the picnic site, and we began to unload and set up the chafing dishes and the other items we had brought. When that was done, I walked over to the big tent and staked our claim to some seats, as Bill basted the pig one last time.

After getting our drinks, I sat down and started up a conversation with Ron Hwilka, another deacon from the church. Ron taught the Men's

Bible Study Class, and I began asking him questions about his classes. He told me he had seven
men in his class on a regular basis. He went on to
say that in another week he would have a mixed
class of men and women.

"Why is that?" I asked.

"Well," he said, "Carolyn Brown (the Women's
Bible Study Class teacher) and her husband have
purchased a new home in Lake Gaston, Virginia,
and he's already moved down to the lake. Tomorrow morning is her last day to teach the class. She's
been trying to find someone to take over the class,
but so far she's had no success."

In my mind I was saying, "God, look at You!
Right on time—without a minute to spare!"

Quickly I responded to Deacon Hwilka, "Ron,
I'm so glad you told me that. I feel God wants me
to teach that class." I couldn't believe my own boldness as I proceeded to tell him about my spiritual
revelations and how God had spoken to me just
a few days before and, again, just within the past
hour.

"Oh ... okay," was Ron's reply, and he kept shaking his head in a positive way. Still I could feel the
unbelief in his actions. I couldn't be sure if he be-

lieved me or not, but it didn't matter. I knew what I knew, and God knew what He knew, and that was all that mattered.

The next day was Sunday again, and I got ready a little early so that I could arrive at the church in time to talk to Carolyn Brown. I got there about fifteen minutes before her class was to begin.

I boldly walked into the Ruth's Love Ladies Adult Bible Study Classroom and asked Carolyn if I could speak with her in private. "Sure," she said, and we stepped into the hallway.

I began telling Carolyn that God had spoken to me audibly, twice, and told me I was to teach, and then Ron had told at the picnic that she was looking for someone to take over her class. He had said that, as of now, she had not found anyone who wanted to do it.

Carolyn began to weep as she spoke. "Sheila," she said, "for nine months now I have searched for someone to take over this class. I have prayed continually for God to send the right person. I have taught the class for many years now, and I didn't want to leave it without a suitable teacher."

Very excited now, she went on: "My husband is already at our new home, and my car is packed beyond belief. I had to stay for final closing on our house, but when church is over today and I pull out of this lot, I'm gone." With that, we fell into each other's arms and hugged and cried.

That was such a God moment. It takes nine months to prepare a baby for birth, and we realized in that moment how perfect God's timing had been. He alone knew what would transpire. It was amazing, just amazing, and our excitement was beyond belief. We knew that God had orchestrated everything, with no time to spare. He was right on time.

Carolyn briefly taught me what I needed to know and then gave me her phone number so I could contact her if any problems came up. We began a correspondence by e-mail and telephone that lasted for about a year. Eventually, however, our lives got too busy, and we drifted apart, but I continued teaching her class. I started that very next Sunday after our agreement, and I could feel a special anointing growing in me as my study in the Word now increased dramatically, and I prepared to do my best at teaching the women of the church.

But when God had said, "You are to teach," He had much more in mind. Because of my obedience in responding to His voice and command, it was absolutely amazing what followed. Within three months of taking over teaching that class at church, I received a phone call from a lady at the College of Southern Maryland asking if I would teach a class on Workforce Development, teaching for a Food Sanitation Certification. I explained to her that although I had been in food service for more than twenty years, I didn't really feel qualified to teach such a class. I had never even taken the class myself.

"Don't worry about that," she said, "we will get you qualified." Sure enough, within three weeks I had received my ServSafe and Prometric Certifications and had received approval to work through both companies as a Proctor for their exams. It was all amazing, just amazing!

Then, about three months later, a lady called me from the University of the District of Columbia (UDC). "Mrs. Kay," she said, "we understand you teach Food Sanitation Certification at the College of Southern Maryland, and we would like you to teach with our Workforce Development program as well." Within weeks, I began teaching at one of the premier schools in the in-

ner city of our nation's capitol, training the un-
derprivileged and under-educated in the southeast area of the city.

I continued to work with Workforce Development for the next fourteen years as Adjunct Professor with UDC, working through three different
campuses—PR Harris in Southeast, Bertie Backus
in Northeast and Shadd on East Capital Street. This
was all quite amazing!

When this happened, doors then opened all
over the capitol city for me to witness to the lost.
Every single day there would be someone who
needed to talk with anyone who was willing to listen, someone in need of friendship and someone
who needed the Lord.

Three months after the initial call from the university, I received another call, this one for another
teaching position with United Planning Organization of Washington, D.C. (They were the creators
of the Head Start program.) They asked if I would
be willing to teach for them too. Within a month I
began teaching for this community outreach organization as well.

How wonderful is our God! He had said, "You
are to teach!" I began in church, and then reached

out into the community. Especially thrilling to me was the fact that this extended to the inner city, where the need for God was beyond belief. He had put me in my element—food service—made a teacher out of me, anointed me to teach, and made me an adjunct professor at colleges and universities (when I had never even completed high school myself). God placed me in positions in which I was paid well, while at the same time I was able to work with thousands upon thousands in serious evangelism. It doesn't get much better than that!

One day a young woman, a student in the three-day class I was teaching at the UPO Center on Good Hope Road in Southeast Washington, came into the classroom a little late. I noticed some swelling and bruising on her face. Her left eye was swollen, and she was visibly lacking the confidence in her step that had been there just the day before. I overheard her tell another student at her table that she had been attacked and raped the night before.

Concerned, I approached her and asked what I could do. She looked at me and said, "Professor Kay, this is the inner city, a place of drunks and drug addicts. Every woman in this room has been raped." I had about thirty students at the time, twenty-four of them women, and just six men.

"If it's not by our fathers, then it's by our brothers, and if it's not by our brother,d then it's by our cousins. If it's not by our cousins, then it's by a neighbor. If it's not by a neighbor, then it's by an uncle. If it's not by an uncle, then it's by a baby sitter or a date. And, Professor, don't think it's just women and young girls; it's the men as well. They were all raped when they were young boys."

I wanted to hear just one man in that room say, "Not me," but I was never able to hear those words.

This conversation brought a river of tears to my eyes, because I knew that every word she had spoken was true. It brought back memories of my own past that I had suppressed and didn't really want to recall.

After the Lord made me a teacher, He also added evangelism to my gifts, and I began working with others in the inner city. We were able to feed the homeless on Saturdays, furnishing them a hot meal while preaching to them the blessings of Christ's cross. We taught them on forgiveness, a new life and eternal salvation. To many, this was not an altogether new message. Most of them had been taught about salvation by their grandmothers when they were children, but their bad decisions in life had led them away from the church.

We would conduct services with the homeless on Sundays, and a handful of them were very faithful about showing up. For others, we had to drive around and pick them up. The coffee and donuts we served were always a good incentive.

We named this ministry Restoring the Broken Vessel. Today we also do special conferences, working with abused woman around the country, teaching the importance of forgiveness and how to love those who have done us wrong.

This calling came to me when I had been sufficiently prepared, and it has grown and matured from there. My personal calling to teach began with those wonderful words spoken to me by God's Spirit: "You are to teach." Then, very quickly, I had become an evangelist. When the Holy Spirit spoke through me to one class, saying, "Get your life straight with God, for time is short," the students wept, and many believed and were saved.

Other gifts developed in my life. Through a dream I will relate in a later chapter, God gave me the gift of prophecy. I had prophesied before, but now I knew this was definitely part of His plan for me. One day He even directed me to have a gathering of the prophets.

Many of my gifts developed while working in the House of Prayer, Prophecy and Healing that the Lord gave me. As I'll show in a later chapter, many other ministers were blessed by this facility to grow their own congregations, and I was able to let them use it without charge. *"You will know them by their fruit"* the Lord told me.

I had several husband-and-wife ministries, one mother-and-daughter ministry, two powerful deliverance ministries and two single ministers who were blessed by utilizing that facility. Three of these minister friends were eventually ordained under the same missionary group I was ordained under. [1] Two of those couples went on to open their own churches, one in La Plata, Maryland and the other in Waldorf. Both deliverance ministries went on to have their own services in rented spaces, one at a hotel in Waldorf and the other on Friday evenings in Clinton, and have continued to advance their

1. Cross Country World Missions of Rocky Mount, North Carolina, under the leadership of the late Anne Baines and Apostle Jessie Blalock.

ministries. In this way, God added church-builder to my list of giftings.

It seems that the Lord is preparing me for the gift of apostleship. Many apostles have told me I have that gift, but I wait to hear it from the Lord's own lips. We never want to puff ourselves up or pretend to be something we are not. An apostle usually carries all five of the ministry gifts. They all begin as disciples, but then, as they are taught by the Holy Spirit, they move from glory, to glory, to glory. That was certainly what was happening to me. I was *Maturing in Sonship through Suffering.* (I'll get to the suffering part soon enough.)

✝ ✝ ✝

How to Worship

Read 1 Chronicles 16:10

Give glory to His holy name.

Give glory to His character.

Give glory to His power.

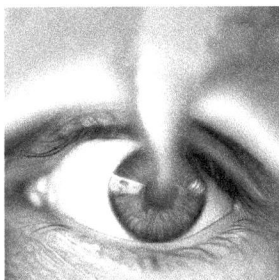

The Eyes Are the Window to the Soul

By him therefore let us offer the sacrifice of praise to God continually, that is, the fruit of our lips giving thanks to his name. But to do good and to communicate forget not; for with such sacrifices God is well pleased.   Hebrew 13:15-16

After meeting the heavenly Jesus, Saul, the ultimate persecutor of the Church, become a Christian, and his life was changed forever. He was now Paul. On the road to Damascus, he had been blinded by brilliant white light from above. The eyes are the window to the soul.

51

Looking back in time, I can relate with Paul, when he said, *"whether in the body, I cannot tell; or whether out of the body, I cannot tell: God knoweth"* (2 Corinthians 12:2), because spiritual revelations can leave you wondering what has happened and why. When it happens, your faith increases by leaps and bounds, almost beyond belief, and you know without a doubt that what you have experienced is real.

It was 2 o'clock in the afternoon, and I was standing in my prayer closet, my eyes closed as I prayed aloud, worshiping the One I love, my Lord and Savior, Jesus Christ. Suddenly, a brilliant bright and beautiful white light (a brilliance beyond description) came as a whirlwind toward me, swirling as it entered like a funnel and was then poured into my right eye.

There was an ever-so-faint hint of color, a pale emerald green interwoven around the outer edge of the top portion of the swirling. This cool refreshing phenomenon, with the appearance of a tornado, transitioned smoothly, without missing a beat in its motion, as it then entered into my left eye.

I embraced this new level of intimacy with the Lord, for it was beautiful and glorious. There was a freshness, a cool refreshing feeling, a peaceful impartation of His love. I suppose it is surprising that I was not at all frightened by this experience. In fact, there was a strange peace that came over me in that moment.

As I said, the light entered my body through my right eye at first, and then, after thirty seconds, smoothly and uninterruptedly, switched over to the left eye for the same period of time. When it exited my eye, it went outward and upward toward the north. My eyes remained closed, but I could see all that was happening.

I kept my eyes closed for at least thirty more seconds and did not try to force them open. I just relaxed and waited on the Lord.

Standing there, not knowing what had just happened, I wanted to continue absorbing the beauty of the moment. The peace and the unbelievable splendor that I felt was truly indescribable. Then, within seconds, my eyes gently opened of their own accord.

That night, after going to sleep, I was awakened at about 3 a.m. by what appeared to be dark, slick mud being thrown from my eyes (both at the same time). It was like sludge, filth, but I could see particles, pieces of unidentifiable sin being thrown out through my eyes. My sin was being purged from my body. I could not identify this sin, nor did I want to. I just knew that all sin was being purged from me.

Once the purging had stopped, my body began to shake. This was not a jerking motion but more like a constant, rhythmical shaking. It reminded me of the movement made by a milkshake machine.

I decided to leave the bedroom, thinking the shaking might wake my husband, so I sat at the kitchen table in prayer. It felt like my body was shaking all over, yet when I raised my right hand and arm out in front of me, I could see that they were not shaking at all. I did the same with each of my legs, checking to see how much they were shaking. As with the arms, my legs were not shaking either. It soon became clear to me that although it felt like I was shaking all over, the shaking was taking place only in the main trunk of my body, my insides. My thought was that the Holy Spirit was preparing a place, a clean pure place, where He could comfortably settle in.

I believed then (and still do believe) that He settled in my left side, just below the rib cage. When

I would lovingly rub that area, I could feel movement, as though a baby was kicking. It was absolutely amazing!

From then on, I felt different, I looked different, and I even acted different. When I went to the grocery store the next day, a woman of color approached me in the main aisle. She seemed nervous and uneasy. "I can't seem to find the baking soda," she said.

"I believe that would be with the cake mixes, flour and baking supplies," I offered. "Would you like me to get it for you?"

"Yes, thank you," she replied.

When I returned in a few minutes with the baking soda in hand, she was standing in the same spot and had begun to cry. "Oh, honey, what's wrong?" I asked, as I reached out to embrace her.

"I've just come from the doctor," she said, "and they said I have brain cancer."

I looked at her and smiled. "The Lord has led you to me today. He wants me to lay hands on you, and a healing will take place, because this is how He works. His power will funnel through me and my faith, into you. Let your faith receive the healing, and you will be healed in the name of Jesus."

"Wow! Where did that come from?" I wondered, as I put my hand on the back of her head where she had indicated the brain tumor was located. I had never been asked to pray for anyone, especially a total stranger, and here we were, standing in the center aisle of the Giant Food store, in Waldorf, Maryland, holding each other, crying and praying for God's intervention and for a manifestation of healing to take place.

I often regret not having gotten that lady's phone number or some other means of follow-up. I never saw her again, but I know what God did that day.

That evening (this was the day after the light entered my eyes, sin was purged from my body and the shaking took place, and after laying hands on a woman with brain cancer), I had books spread out all over my kitchen table, as I began a study on the subject of prophecy for my Sunday Bible study class. As I flipped through my *Webster's Bible Dictionary*, searching for the word *prophecy*, for some reason my eyes fell on the word *prostitute*. With all the many spiritual revelations I'd had prior to this, I was never frightened, but when my eyes fell on that word *prostitute*, my head turned away instantly, and my eyes diverted to the left. I had not turned my head; it was turned for me!

What was so frightening to me was that the Holy Spirit could not look upon that word. Sin had been purged from my body. I now had no desire to even watch television, people suddenly seemed drawn to me as never before, and now my head was being turned so that I would not look upon words that, in any way, spoke of sin. How frightening! *In today's world, how could that be avoided?* I wondered.

The following Sunday, after teaching my Bible study class, I joined Bill in the sanctuary for the morning service. Suddenly, the Holy Spirit spoke to me saying, "Go to Cedarville and lay hands on a man with prostate cancer. Go now!"

I looked over at Bill and asked, "Where is Cedarville?"

He said it was about fifteen minutes away, and told me how to get there. "Why?" he asked.

I swallowed hard before I answered, "God has asked me to go there and lay hands on a man with prostate cancer."

"Sheila," he said, "don't let people hear you talk like that. They'll think you're crazy." (Satan was using own husband to plant doubt in my mind.)

"Do *you* think I'm crazy?" I asked him.

"No!" he said, "but how are you going to know who has prostate cancer in a place where you don't even know people?"

"Where is your faith, Oh mighty man of God?" I thought to myself, but my response to him was, "Honey, don't you think if God sends me, He will also show me who has the cancer?" Having said that, I excused myself and got up to follow God's instructions.

We must free ourselves of unbelief and hardness of heart. We must believe, have faith. Jesus said, *"They shall lay hands on the sick, and they shall recover"* (Mark 16:18). It is not the hands, nor the anointing oil that is often used that will bring forth healing, but faith in God. I had to be obedient to what I had heard.

The first church I came to in Cedarville was the local Assembly of God. It was situated on the left side of the road. I noticed that there were huge power lines crossing over the property. Across from the church was a pond, and there were several cows grazing in the field.

I parked and went into the church and was seated by one of the smiling deacons. "Good morning," he said, "what brings you here today?"

"The Holy Spirit brought me here this morning," I replied.

He smiled and said, "Well, that's wonderful!"

I thought to myself, "If you only knew what transpired in our Baptist church this morning."

I sat down and began to pray, "Okay, Lord, I'm here. Now please show me what I'm to do."

I watched as the keyboard player came out onto the platform and began playing some soft background music. He paused for a brief moment, and then he began to speak, as he resumed the soft playing.

"I want to thank those of you who have sent cards and flowers and have brought meals to our home," the man said. "And most of all, for your calls to my wife, and for your prayers."

Feeling a sudden spurt of boldness, I stood and said, "Excuse me, brother, but could you tell me what's wrong with you?"

With that, everything went silent. Every head in the church turned my way, and everyone stared at me. The piano player also just stared at me. I could hear him thinking, "Who are you? And do I want to tell you what's wrong with me?"

"I have prostate cancer," he finally answered.

"No!" I said. "You *had* prostate cancer. God has sent me here this morning to lay hands on you. He wants you healed. His anointing will flow to you through my hands."

It took only an instant for him to run across the platform, grab a bottle of anointing oil, and run down the aisle to where I stood. The twenty-five or so people who were in the church came and gathered around us, many reaching out their hands toward us. Some touched me, and others laid hands on him.

He handed me the bottle of anointing oil. After putting some of the oil on my fingertips. I touched his forehead and said, "In the name of Jesus Christ of Nazareth, you are healed!"

Again, healing is not in the oil, and it's not in the words. It's in the faith. From the moment the man had heard my words and believed, from the moment he had picked up the anointing oil and run down the aisle of the church toward me, his faith had been in motion.

My faith had gone into motion when I heard the Lord speak to me and I believed. Although Satan had tried to discourage me through my husband, I had persevered in faith. Now my faith joined with the sick man's faith and brought the needed healing.

And that was it. I had done what I was called to do. The man returned to the keyboard, and I picked up my Bible and purse and left for home. As I drove, the Lord spoke to me, "Only lay hands on people when I tell you to. Then you will know they are healed."

Several years later, I returned to that Assembly of God Church and learned that the young man I had prayed for had been the pastor's son. Pastor Johnson had since died, and a new pastor had taken over the church. The keyboard player, Pastor Johnson's son, was still alive and well, with no signs of the cancer, but he, too, had moved on to another church.

That afternoon I took time to explain to my husband everything that had been happening with my spiritual revelations to that point. As a retired State Police investigator and barrack commander, he'd had a questioning spirit. That was okay with me, because that was who he was. I felt better now because the door had been opened and whenever strange things happened to me, I knew I could tell Bill about it. Whether he always believed me or not I can't say, but it was obvious to him that there was a complete change in me, my way of life, and my love for the Lord.

This was all building his faith in the things of the Bible, and he was open now to hearing about the gifts of the Spirit (which he had always been taught were only for the New Testament Church during Bible times and not for today).

The rest of my family also saw the dramatic change in me. I was a different person. Bill knew that God had changed me forever and that our life would never be the same again. He saw my hunger and unquenchable thirst for the Lord and my constant study of His Word. He knew the Lord was my life and that I longed to be holy as He is holy.

I was now a creature of praise and could offer unto God the sacrifice of praise continually:

By him therefore let us offer the sacrifice of praise to God continually, that is, the fruit of our lips giving thanks to his name. But to do good and to communicate forget not; for with such sacrifices God is well pleased. Hebrews 13:15-16

We serve a mighty God, and none can compare with Him! I was *Maturing in Sonship through Suffering.* (Yes, I'll get to the suffering part.)

How to Worship

Read 1 Chronicles 16:11

Seek the Lord.

Seek His strength.

Seek His face.

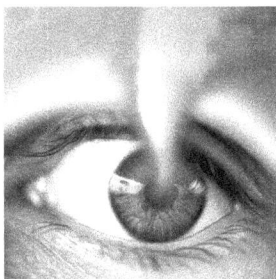

~ FOUR ~

An Unction Saves a Life

But, ye have an unction from the Holy One, and ye know all things.   1 John 2:20

There were just two days left before the kids would be out of school for the summer. That day the twelve-year-olds of the girl's softball team were having their final game. Jodie, my youngest daughter, and Chrissy, her best friend, were playing.

The snack bar was getting ready to close, and hot dogs, pizza and drinks were all reduced to half price. I made my way over to take advantage of the sale and surprise the kids with a snack.

Just then the game ended. Jodie spotted me, and she and Chrissy came running toward me, relieving me of trying to juggle the sodas and dogs.

"Mom," Jodie said, "Chrissy's mom invited me to go with them to West Virginia, to spend two weeks on their grandmother's farm. They have a wonderful farm, with chickens, cows, pigs and two horses that we can ride. Please, Mom, can I go? Please! Please! Please!" She was very excited about the prospect.

Chrissy was excited as well, thinking that Jodie might go, and joined in, "They don't smoke or drink. All they do is go to church, feed the animals and sit on the porch. Please, can she go? We'll have such a great time."

The girls didn't realize it, but from the moment they had begun talking about this trip, my stomach had been tied in knots, as if someone had a tightened fist in my gut. It was what I considered a warning sign or an "unction" from the Holy Spirit. He was warning me of danger, and He was telling me, "No!"

The Word of God tells us:

But ye have an unction from the Holy One, and ye know all things. 1 John 2:20

Jodie was waiting for my answer.

"I don't know, honey," I said. "Let me think about it. I'll talk to Chrissy's mom before I make a decision. Then I'll let you know." That was my response, but I already knew the Lord was telling me not to let Jodie go.

The next morning I called Chrissy's mom, as I had promised I would. She assured me the girls would be in good hands and would have a great time. She would be driving them there herself and picking them up in two weeks. Still, that feeling of apprehension was there, even stronger now, telling me not to let Jodie go.

"I don't know why," I finally told Chrissy's mom, "but God is telling me not to let Jodie go. I wouldn't be comfortable going against this feeling, because it's so very strong. Thank you so much for the invitation and the great opportunity, but at this time, I must say no."

I was certainly not looking forward to telling Jodie she wouldn't be going. Unfortunately she'd never had this type of adventurous opportunity before, a vacation on a farm, and with her best friend. Wow! It doesn't get much better than that, does it?

67

Needless to say, Jodie was very upset, not only because she couldn't go, but also because Chrissy had invited another close friend to go with her, and her parents were letting her go. I'm certain that, at that moment, she felt she had the worst mother in the whole world. But I couldn't help it.

Jodie was very sad, and my heart was breaking over her sadness. She had always been such a good child, and my heart was broken because hers was broken. But I knew what I felt, and I knew I could not let her go.

When the two weeks of the vacation were up, and the day Chrissy's family had scheduled to return had come and gone, I asked Jodie if she had heard from Chrissy since she got back. She said she didn't think they were back yet. Later that morning I went to the mailbox to retrieve our local newspaper, *The Maryland Independent*. The front page told the story. In the photos, the car Chrissy's family had been traveling in was unrecognizable.

It seemed that a trash truck had run into the rear of the car, the gasoline tank had exploded, and the car had been engulfed with flames. All of the occupants of the vehicle were trapped inside and were burned to death in a fiery inferno, with the exception of Chrissy's younger sister, who was pulled from the front passenger seat. She had been flown to the burn center at Children's Hospital in critical condition. A ten-year-old girl, she was covered with third-degree burns over sixty percent of her body, and she was also now without her mother and siblings who had died in that inferno.

As you can imagine, Jodie was upset beyond belief when she heard about the accident and the loss of her best friend and her family. What upset her even more was realizing that she could have been trapped in that back seat in that blazing inferno. She said to me, "Mom, I will never get mad at you again when you say you have a feeling I shouldn't do something, and I will never get mad at God when He warns you of danger. Mom, I'm so sorry I got mad at you and didn't speak to you. I'm sorry! I'm so sorry!" She was sobbing out of control, and I held her close, not wanting to ever let her go.

It was a deeply emotional moment for me too, realizing that my baby girl could have been gone forever, burned to death, trapped in that car. And that's precisely what would have happened if God had not forewarned me, and if I had not listened to that nudge, or feeling of tightness in my stomach. I cannot stress enough the importance of listening to the words or nudges of God. *"Man shall not live buy bread alone"* (Matthew 4:4).

Thank You, Lord! Oh, Father, I praise Your holy name. I will praise You forever, and I will serve You every day of my life!

Jodie and I went to the funeral. There were three bodies, the mother and two of her children, in one closed casket, while the other child remained in critical condition in the hospital with third-degree burns. The crowd was massive in the Huntt Funeral Home in Waldorf, and there was not a dry eye in the place. How could I ever find the words to thank God enough? I would spend my life serving Him.

What words could I use to thank God for saving my child from such a horrific death by forewarning me? What words could I use to tell Him how much I loved Him? I will be eternally grateful to Him for saving my daughter's life.

God didn't spare His own Son, but gave Him for my life. How can I ever thank Him enough? It will take me an eternity and beyond to thank Him.

Lord, I will worship You forever. I will praise You and serve You the rest of my life. I surrender my life to You. I bow before You, Lord, today, tomorrow and forever. Nothing I could do would be enough to repay You for all You have done for me. I worship You, for You are holy. I long to be holy, as You are holy. I will serve You all the days of my life. Lord.

Lord, I know you have saved my daughter for a purpose. It was done for her and for me, for us both. Now we have a bond that will never be broken. Only she and I knew of the warning God had given me. How could I tell others we had been forewarned?

God's Word declares:

To obey is better than sacrifice.   1 Samuel 15:22

I was *Maturing in Sonship through Suffering.*

71

† ✝ †

How to Worship

---

1 Chronicles 16:12

Worship Him

By remembering His Word,

His Works,

And, most of all,

His love.

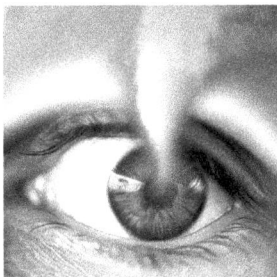

A New Name Written Down in Glory

To him that overcometh, will I give to eat of the hidden manna, and will give him a white stone, and in the stone a new name written, which no man knoweth. Revelation 2:17

How wonderful are Your ways, Oh God!
How wonderful are Your ways.

In Genesis, the book of beginnings, Genesis, the seedbed of all biblical doctrine, Genesis, the book where doctrine can be found in an embryonic form, somewhere in this beginning book of the Bible, the foundation of all and every truth had its beginning.

Early one morning, while sitting at my kitchen table doing a study of Genesis, this fascinating first book of the Old Testament, I started reading about Abram and Sarai for the seventh or eighth time. Genesis had become one of my favorite Bible books. This day, it seemed that I was drawn there again, specifically to the introduction to Abram.

I began reading Genesis 17, where God made covenant with Abram and changed his name to Abraham, simply by adding an H and an A. Strangely that had slipped past me before. I knew of the name change, but had never given much notice as to what letters were added.

The same was true for Sarah. God said to Abraham, *"As for Sarai thy wife, thou shalt not call her name Sarai, but Sarah shall her name be"* (verse 15). An H and an A were placed at the end of her name, and she became Sarah. Then, in Genesis 18:12, I read, *"Sarah laughed."* After noticing that an H and an A had been added to the end of their names and then Sarah had laughed, I too began to laugh. Ha! Ha!

"Lord, You are so funny," I said, as my laughter grew louder. "You are just so very funny."

I knew that the name of Isaac, the son born to Abraham and Sarah, meant laughter, and now I looked at the HA added to Abraham's name and the AH added to Sarah's name, and I realized that it spelled *ha*! That was laughter, and that was their son's name. How funny! I laughed some more.

"God, You have the best sense of humor," I said, as I began laughing again.

Softly, I heard Him speak to me inwardly. He was saying, "And I have changed your name, too." I could almost hear a smile in His voice as He said this.

"Lord, what have You changed it to?" I asked.

He answered, "Write your name."

Quickly I grabbed a pad and pen and wrote my first name: S H E I L A.

"Now what do you see?" God asked.

"I see Sheila," was my reply.

"Write it again," He said.

So I wrote my first name again: S H E I L A.

"What do you see?" He asked again.

Once again I answered, "Sheila."

"Write your name again," He said.

For the third time, I wrote S H E I L A.

"What do you see?" God asked. This time, as I looked at the name SHEILA and began to speak it, I was amazed to see that the letters in my name began to move slowly right before my eyes. They moved one at a time, very methodically.

First the I moved behind the L, and then the S moved behind the I. After that the S and H moved together between the I and the A, spelling out my new name, a name that God had personally given me—ELISHA. He had used every letter in my given name to give me a new name.

ELISHA ... When I saw it, I began to laugh again. My new name also ended with H and A. Just as God had changed the name of Abram and Sarai, He had also changed my name.

I read in Revelation:

To him that overcometh will I give to eat of the hidden manna, and will give him a white stone, and on the stone a new name written, which no man knoweth save he that receiveth it.

Revelation 2:17

I decided to buy a flat white stone, have ELISHA engraved on it and wear it around my neck forever as a reminder of what the Lord had done.

My focus now became a study of Elijah and El-isha, and I immediately noticed that Elisha had the H A, as did Abraham, and Elijah had the A H, as did Sarah. I personally found that to be fascinating.

Recently a minister from Africa's Ivory Coast came to one of our meetings. We were holding a Prayer, Prophecy and Healing service at my place of worship, and Rev. Aniebe listened intently as I told the story of my name being change to Elisha. "Why aren't you using this name given you by God?" he asked. "This is not a daily occurrence. You must feel very honored."

Yes, it is an honor and a privilege to use a name God Himself has given you. Names are important to God, and they're important to me as well.

My father, Leo Emmett Goldberg, was Jewish. The few of his immediate family on the Goldberg side who escaped the Holocaust moved to this country and lived on Cherry Street in New York City, down by the waterfront. In the Old Country, the family had lived in Goldberg, Germany, which sits beside the lake of the same name.

Many of the Goldbergs were slaughtered by Hitler's regime. They were starved to death, gassed in the camps, beaten to death, or striped naked and forced to parade through the streets before they were shot or buried alive (still in their nakedness). For some, every bone was visible when they died.

Those bones will one day cry out from the grave. I hope the Lord has me speak out over those bones one day, for I long to see them come to life. As the daughter of a Holocaust survivor, I learned at an early age what hate, prejudice, cultural differences and religious intolerance could do to a people, a nation or even the whole world.

Dad's mother and her side of the family lived in Leavenworth, Kansas. But all I know about my grandfather on Dad's side is that he was shot to death there in Kansas when Dad was just a lad. This would have been between 1913 and 1920. My grandfather had worked in the coal mines, and I believe he was killed because of his Jewish faith.

Dad dropped out of school and joined the military when he was just fifteen. His mom, Minnie (Turley) Goldberg, signed for him, saying he was already sixteen. The war was in full swing in Germany and Poland, and our forces were preparing to invade, so they were recruiting anyone who could carry a gun.

Grandmother Goldberg had grown up extremely poor, often going without food, and forced to move from here to there or, as the old saying goes, "from pillar to post." If Dad were to die in the war, this would give her a means of support through a government pension.

Dad stayed in the U.S. Navy for thirty-four years, retiring as a Lt. Commander. He served as an electrical engineer. He then joined the Civil Service, working with the Navy for many additional years here at home.

A few years after Dad returned from the war, he called for a family gathering: Mom, my sister Jean and I (we were just small children at the time). "I'm going to change our last name," he announced. "I have already seen a lawyer about it. A notice will run in the paper for a few days, and that will be it."

"Why, Daddy? Why would you change our name?" I remember hearing Jean, all of seven years old, ask.

"Well," he answered, "Sheila is having a difficult time spelling Goldberg. Turley will be easier for her to spell." And that was that. A few weeks later, the change was official. I could spell Turley and was able to get my library card, never giving the matter any more thought. So I grew up as Sheila Turley.

As years went by, I began to realize that the reason Dad had done this was much more complex than he had led us to believe. He had been persecuted throughout his time in the military. The men her served with called him "Little Jew Boy." He was also called "Goldie." I remember asking him one day, "Daddy, why do they call you Goldie?"

He said it was because he had a gold tooth (which he did), but I knew better. It was because his last name was Goldberg, and these men had a prejudice against Jewish people.

Dad had seen what happened to his family members, and he was part of the war going on now, so he saw hatred and persecution firsthand and at its worst. It stripped people of their dignity, their heritage and their pride. Dad never practiced his Jewish faith again and never mentioned to anyone that he was Jewish.

Israel had now become a nation, and many Jews were fleeing there, but somehow Dad could not foresee things getting better. So, wanting the best for me, my sister and mother in the future, he changed our name, hoping that no one would guess that we were Jewish. He did not want us to be persecuted, as he and our ancestors had been before us.

Today, if he were living, I would first thank my father for having loved me and for wanting to protect me, but I would also let him know that I am not happy that he sold his birthright. I want my name back, and at a certain point, I began taking it back, using it as my own. He had given away a name of promise in exchange for a name of poverty.

When my Jewish name was taken from me, my heritage was taken from me. But by changing my name from Sheila to Elisha, Almighty God had restored to me my Jewish heritage.

Thank You, Lord! I did not see that until I began writing this page. Lord, You have given my Jewish heritage back to me. I honor You, Father, and I honor my daddy. Thank You that I was able to lead him to the cross before he died. Lord, I give You praise.

Amen!

Elisha

I was *Maturing in Sonship through Suffering.*

How to Worship

Give unto the Lord

All the glory due

His name.

When there is a moving of the

Spirit in the house,

All we must do is to bring

Honor and glory to the Lord!

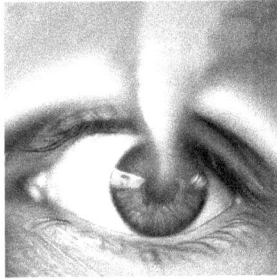

~ SIX ~

A Prophetic Vision

The voice of thy brother's blood crieth unto Me from the ground. And now art thou cursed from the earth, which hath opened her mouth to receive thy brother's blood from thy hand.

Genesis 4:10-11

The word *vision* can be defined as: "something being seen, visible, to discern clearly, to experience, to appear, to behold, to perceive, to see, to take heed, to gaze with eyes wide open at something remarkable, to observe." It also refers to "mystery removed, being revealed, remove the covering, forewarning." It is the unveiling of things not known before, which God alone could make known.

83

God was not pleased with Cain when he killed his brother, and he pronounced a curse upon any man who sheds his brother's blood:

Whoso sheddeth man's blood, by man shall his blood be shed; for in the image of God made He man. Genesis 9:6

It was September 9, 2001, and Bill and I had gone to a Sunday evening Bible Study at the First Baptist Church of St. Charles. Pastor Bill was teaching that night. I don't remember what part of the Bible we were studying in that class, but what I do remember will forever be deeply inscribed in my subconscious.

Pastor Bill was an excellent teacher, and he kept our attention. I was listening intently to what he was saying, and I was also watching him closely as he spoke. Then a sudden movement diverted my attention, and my head turned in the direction of that movement.

There was a large beautifully-varnished wooden cross that hung over the baptismal pool, and it was illuminated from behind. With my left peripheral vision, I could now see blood dripping heavily from that cross. I turned fully in that direction and heard our pastor say, "Sheila, what's wrong? You're as white as a ghost."

"Pastor," I said, "I know it isn't real, but I see blood dripping from the cross. It's running down into the baptismal pool." It was not just a small amount of blood. There was a lot of it. Now everyone in the sanctuary turned to look at that big cross.

What I was seeing was so real that I was tempted to go look in the pool and see how much blood was in there, but I thought better of it.

"Sheila," Pastor Bill said, "God has given you a vision."

"But what does it mean, Pastor Bill?" I asked.

"I don't know," he responded. "God sometimes gives visions as a warning of something that will be in the near future. This might represent an event that will take place. Visions can be unusual and bizarre reminders of sin, or they can be unique as the dry bones in Ezekiel. Daniel also had many prophetic visions. Most visions are telling of retaliation for sin, but not all."

That happened at about 7 p.m. on Sunday evening. By the morning of Tuesday, which was September 11, 2001, the blood of thousands of innocent victims began seeping into the ground under the first of the fallen Twin Towers in New York City, and it continued to seep as the second tower also fell. It was all the work of radical Islamists from the Middle East. Since then the blood of God's children has cried out to Him from that ground.

Within hours, blood also began seeping into the ground in a field on Lamb Shank Road in Pennsylvania, and that blood again cried out to God from the ground. This was the case where American heroes took back control of the plane from the radicals and caused it to dive nose first into that field to prevent the intended attack on the U.S. Capital in Washington, D.C.

Still another plane got through and crashed into the Pentagon, the headquarters of our military located in Alexandria, Virginia, across the river from the nation's Capitol. Blood again seeped into the ground, crying out to God.

Each of these planes was used as a guided missiles in well-planned acts of terrorism, because of men's hatred and objection to our faith.

That evening, Pastor Bill called and asked, "Sheila, do you see the connection of your vision with what has just taken place in New York City?"

"Yes, Pastor," I answered. I do." The blood had flowed from above (as from the cross) and into the ground below (as into the baptismal pool). And, as Abel's blood had cried out to God from the ground in years past, so the blood of many slaughtered innocents is crying out even today, as brother continues to kill brother.

Pastor Bill said, "God gave the vision, knowing you could not stop what was about to happen, Sheila, but so that you would know He is an all-knowing God who is still on the throne and in total control. We cannot second-guess God. We, as a country, have turned our backs on Israel. We have killed millions of babies through abortion (throwing them into trash cans), while the Christian Church sleeps, and continues to make many mistakes of their own, as has our government. We have turned our back on our fellowman and on God ... ," (he paused) "... looking for that feel-good religion that psychology offers."

He continued, "Sheila, God has chosen you to see this vision. I find that to be remarkable in itself. Perhaps it was because of the fact that you are the only Jewish person in our congregation. Perhaps it was to draw you closer to Him. You will one day know the purpose, but not today."

Paul wrote that he refused to boasts in *"visions and revelations"* (2 Corinthians 12:1). Again a vision is "the unveiling of things not known before, and which God alone could make known."

The Hebrew words translated *vision* can be variously described as "a sight, look, vision, dream, revelation, oracle, agreement, notable, the act of seeing, appearance, to look upon, pattern, to see, sight, a mirror, looking glass, a seer." The Greek word translated as *vision* explains it as "visually, an apparition, something gazed at, especially supernatural, the act of gazing, an inspired appearance, sight, vision."

The words *vision* or *visions* occur more than one hundred times in the Bible. The most frequent Old Testament word is *chazown*, and in the New Testament, the word most often used is *horama*. Visions should not be a strange thing for us. As Spirit-filled believers, we should expect to have them. Thank God I was *Maturing in Sonship through Suffering*.

✝ ✝ ✝

How to Worship

We are the

Watchmen,

The changing

Of the

Guard.

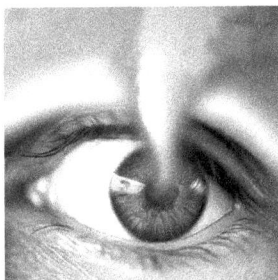

~ SEVEN ~

Forgiveness Saved My Life

*If ye forgive not men their trespasses, neither will
your Father forgive your trespasses.*

Matthew 6:15

It was closing time at the Bath Boutique in
Portsmouth, Virginia, where I was working as assistant manager. I went by the bank and made a
deposit in the drop box, as was our regular proce-
dure on Sunday evenings.

The weather was beautiful, and the sun was
beginning to go down on that late spring evening,
so I lowered the top on my red Ford Fairlane con-
vertible, just wanting to feel refreshed from the
wind as it blew through my long hair. Anticipat-

ing this pleasure, I had removed the barrette that had held my hair neatly back in a professional style during my work hours, and now it was free to blow.

As I slowed for a red traffic light, I noticed four young men crossing the street from my left. I reached forward to adjust the radio station, to get a clearer sound, when suddenly I was sucker punched from my left, lifted and then tossed into the rear seat. The four men jumped into the car and roared off, not bothering to open a door. I was not unconscious, but I was stunned, and blood trickled down between my eyes.

"Hey, man, let me off at the next corner," the teenager in the front passenger seat said. "Let me out, man! I want no part of this!"

"Lord, protect me! Lord protect me," I kept repeating to myself in horror. "Please, Lord, help me!" I continually said this under my breath, never speaking a word to my assailants.

What transpired next I can't say for sure. I'm not certain if God blocked my memory of it, or if I was unconscious or just why I can't remember it. But I'm glad I don't. The next thing I do remember is being gang-raped over and over by the three remaining men, for what seemed like an eternity. My clothes had been ripped from my body, and I was lying on the ground about fifteen feet from the car.

We were in an lonely wooded area. In the background I could hear a dog barking. For some reason, I thought I had been driven to a rural area in Chesapeake, Virginia, near the General Electric plant. But I couldn't be certain.

The sound of the barking dog seemed to be getting closer ... until one of the men said, "Let's get out of here, man. Someone's coming."

I was punched in the face on my left jaw one last time, and this left me semi-conscious. Then I vaguely remember being choked, at which point I passed out, although in the haze of the moment, I did remember hearing the men running off into the woods.

When regained consciousness, I lay there very still for a while, afraid to move a muscle. I somehow felt the men were hiding in the woods, waiting to see if I was still alive. It seemed as if I lay there for an eternity.

Finally, not hearing any more movement, and keeping my body as still as possible, I began sliding one hand around over the ground as far as I could reach, feeling for any of my clothing. Then gradually, I turned to my left and very slowly pulled myself up into a sitting position, listening all the while for any further movement.

Eventually I felt safe enough to continue the search for my clothes. I was able to find my elastic waist skirt and then my blouse. I never did find my under garments.

As I continued searching, I found my shoes. Finding my car keys ... that was the best find yet.

I got in the car as quietly as possible, started it up and, keeping the lights off, slowly backed out of the wooded area.

"Lord, don't let them see me!" I prayed. "Don't let them see me! Please, help me, Lord! Don't let them be on this road! Lord, help me, please!"

Then, as I gained ground, my despair turned to rejoicing. The violence of the attack had convinced me that the men fully intended to kill me so that I could never identify them. "Oh, my God, I'm free! I'm alive! Oh, my God! Oh, God, thank You! Thank You!"

Now I was crying out loud: "Thank You, Lord! Thank You, Lord! Thank You!"

I didn't feel completely safe yet. "Lord, don't let them find me," I remember praying. "Please don't let them have my purse or my address."

Then I began praying that I wouldn't catch a red light and have to stop again. "Lord, don't make me stop at a red light. Let all my lights be green. Thank You, Lord! Thank You! Thank You."

When I finally pulled into the driveway of my home, I began searching the car, looking for my purse. My shoes were on the floor in the back seat, where I had been tossed like a rag doll. "Oh great! I found my purse on the passenger side of the front seat."

I began to brush the dirt and pine needles from my matted hair. Searching in the glove compartment, I found some baby wipes and began wiping the blood from my face, mouth and forehead. With another cloth, I wiped my arms and legs.

As I approached the door, I could see my babysitter sleeping on the couch. Amy lived directly across the street from our house and was a great help when I had to work. My husband and I had separated several months before, and my two youngest children, Jodie and Jeffrey, were in bed asleep.

Amy had a small night light on, and I didn't want any more light to be turned on that might reveal the cuts and bruises on my face. Thank goodness she was groggy and never noticed.

I watched Amy as she crossed the street, and I waited for her to enter her house and turn off the porch light. Once I knew she was safe inside, I immediately pulled the drapes shut and went to make sure all the doors—front, back and garage—were locked securely. Then I searched my wallet, to make sure the men had not taken anything with my address on it. I was surprised to find that they hadn't taken anything at all. This wasn't about robbery; it was all about rape and murder.

I looked in on the children. They seemed to be sleeping peacefully enough. Then, as quickly as I could, I grabbed a towel and wash cloth and made my way to the shower.

I have no idea how long I stayed in the shower that night, but it seemed as if I somehow couldn't get clean enough. I scrubbed and scrubbed until my skin felt raw. I washed my hair over and over, trying to get the leaves and dirt out that seemed to be embedded in my scalp.

Finally I gave up, dried off, put on my robe and slippers, and went to put the towels in the dirty clothes hamper. Then I began double-checking all the doors again, thinking the men might have somehow entered the house while I was in the shower.

Next I went back to check on the children again, even looking in their closets. I went back to make sure all the security lights were turned on outside. This included those in the backyard, the front yard, and the light in the garage.

Then, going tentatively into my bedroom, I began checking in the closets, looking behind the doors, and getting down on my hands and knees to make sure no one was hiding under the bed.

It suddenly dawned on me that I didn't have to work the next day. I was so grateful. I was an emotional wreck.

I was in and out of sleep all that night, and by morning I knew that I could not stay in that area. I called my boss and said that there had been a family emergency and that I would be leaving the area for a while.

I called my parents, who were living in Maryland, and asked if I could come and stay with them until I could find another job. They had known that my husband and I had separated and had asked me to come home several months earlier. I didn't tell them why I needed to come home now. I didn't tell them I had been raped. They would have insisted I call the police. But I had no intention of going through years of court proceedings and having my name and photo in the newspapers. I could not put myself or my children through that. I was too private a person.

I never did tell my parents what happened that night—or anyone else for that matter. It would only have caused them further stress and made them worry about me even more.

Twenty-two years later, when I was about to re-marry, to a wonderful Christian man named Bill Kay, was the first time I ever mentioned to anyone about being gang-raped. I thought it was only fair to him that I be honest and upfront about the experience before he married me.

Bill was very understanding and sympathetic about what had happened. He also understood why I had wanted to leave that area and why I chose not to press charges.

Although I felt I had done the right thing by not divulging this secret to anyone, I had suffered the emotional consequences. I had suppressed my feelings for so many years that I was now filled with hatred toward my assailants.

But it went far beyond that. I was always jumpy when anyone touched me or tried to hug me. That dreadful experience had affected me in ways I had never understood before. I had built walls around myself, afraid of letting anyone get too close.

I now felt the Lord was working with me in many ways on my need to forgive anyone and everyone who had ever hurt me. He was teaching me about the fruit of the Spirit. I realized that I would never grow in grace and my walk with Him would always be distant until I forgave others, as He had forgiven me. I also knew that Jesus had died to take upon Himself my sins. That evening, during my prayer time, I asked the Lord to forgive those young men and to bring anyone else who had ever come against me in any way to my memory so that I could forgive them as well.

Several days later the Lord spoke to me clearly, "You asked Me to forgive them. You are the one who must forgive." When I realized I had not forgiven them, I began to pray differently. My prayer now was: "Lord, my God, I forgive those who came against me and beat and raped me. I forgive them completely. And, Lord, I ask for their salvation." I continued to pray this prayer daily—morning and evening.

One evening, after I had offered this prayer, I suddenly felt as if the weight of the world had been lifted from my shoulders. I felt so clean and forgiven, and I knew without a doubt that I had forgiven everyone who had ever hurt me. I even forgave my first husband for the death of our son (more on this later).

A few days passed, and I heard the Lord say, "Give a blood drive." The next day I went to my pastor and asked if I could use the multipurpose room at the church for a blood drive. He agreed that it would be a great community gesture and told me to let him know the date, so we could involve the whole church. We held the blood drive two weeks later, on a Monday and Tuesday. Before it was over, I gave blood too.

Two weeks later I received a letter from the Red Cross marked "Personal and Confidential." I had been working for a local chapter for more than twenty years. I was extremely active with Disaster Relief Services, was a trained ERV (Emergency Response Vehicle) driver, and had opened many emergency shelters. I was a shelter manager in Slidell, Louisiana, after Katrina.

I wasn't sure what might be in the letter and I hadn't given it much thought. It could just be an invitation to an awards ceremony. When I finally opened the letter and read it, I was shocked. It said: *"Contact your personal physician immediately. Your blood sample shows that you have a sexually transmitted disease (STD). If not treated immediately, this disease could be deadly."*

Within a minute I had grabbed my purse, and with the letter in hand I was out the door. My doctor's office was only fifteen minutes away, and that's where I was headed now.

Fortunately the doctor took me in immediately. She had read the Red Cross report, and she immediately started me on the needed medication. She said she was also sending me for further tests.

I asked her how this could have happened and told her about the gang rape. But that had been so long ago.

"Sheila," she said, "this type of STD can lay dormant for up to thirty years without raising its head. Have Bill come in too, and I'll run some tests on him, just to make sure he hasn't caught it from you."

The rape had occurred some twenty-five years before this, and in that moment, I was so glad I had told my husband all about it. But the whole thing bothered me. "Lord," I prayed, "why didn't You just heal me? Why did I have to learn this through a blood donation?"

His answer was very striking: "Had I healed you, then you would never have known you had the disease in the first place. If you had never forgiven those who hurt you, then you would never have been asked to give the blood drive. And you would not have been healed. "

The fact that I had forgiven my assailants and asked God for their salvation brought me healing. Forgiveness healed me! Praise God!

It is so important that we listen for the voice of God. We must clean up our inner thoughts and take control over our minds. Stop chattering so much and sit in the presence of God. Pray without ceasing. Find a harmony of spirit and soul.

We must learn to identify God's voice, love Him deeper each day, desire to know Him personally, and seek Him above all else.

My prayer now was:

Lord, You are the God who healed me, and I ask You, as Jesus did, **"Father, forgive them; for they know not what they do"** *(Luke 23:34).*

Bill's test came back negative, and my condition responded to the medications. We all have so much to learn. For my part, I was *Maturing in Sonship through Suffering.*

✝ ✝ ✝

How to Worship

Read 1 Chronicles 16:31

Let the heavens be glad,

And let the earth rejoice;

And let men say

Among the nations,

GOD REIGNS!

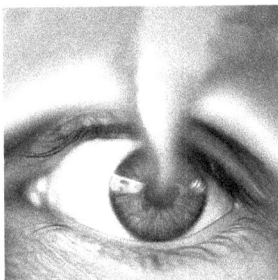

~ EIGHT ~

One Step at a Time

For Mine house shall be called an house of prayer
for all people. Isaiah 56:7

"I will teach you,"saith the Lord, "
And you shall teach others.
And it shall be called a House of Prayer."

After twenty-six years of Christ-filled marriage, the love of my life, my husband Bill, went
home to be with the Lord. He had been retired
from the Maryland State Police when we married, and in retirement, he loved to cook and
clean and had learned to iron his clothes in the
military. In short, he was every wife's dream.

I rarely had to cook when I came home from work.

Bill had been raised in a good old-fashion Christian country home, so he farmed, cleaned, cooked, and helped in all areas of the home, as well as in the field. He would can tomatoes and green beans for days on end. We had a very special bond, and I missed him dearly.

I had long worked as a food-service director in a large veterans' home, at nuclear power plants, and also with colleges, universities, prisons, convention centers and in general catering. Because of our joint love and passion for food service, Bill and I had decided to open a few mobile kitchens and a catering business. He ran the mobile kitchens, and worked special county fairs and contract services, and I ran the catering business, doing weddings and other special events.

But then God had called me to teach and continued to open door after door in that direction. He had first used my food service experience to open doors at colleges and then universities in the inner city. This was all preparing me for ministry, one step at a time.

A week after Bill's death, I went out to the catering kitchen that was in the backyard of our property. As I sat there, remembering all the good times we'd had together, I began to cry. "What am I to do, Lord?" I prayed. "I really don't want to run this business without my husband. Tell me what to do."

Within a minute, God answered me clearly, "It shall be called a house of prayer." I understood that I was to turn the large kitchen into a place for people to gather and seek God. As I looked around the kitchen, the Lord gave me the complete vision. I could see the completed layout of His new House of Prayer.

The next day I put Bill's van up for sale, then the chafing dishes, stoves, racks, pot racks and all the other furnishings of a catering kitchen. I went to the local Lowes and Home Depot and got carpet and tile samples and then compared paint chips to match the colors of the tile and carpet I liked. God has always amazed me how He orchestrates things, and this was truly amazing!

While I was in Lowes, I ran into an old friend from years before, an Amish man from Lancaster, Pennsylvania. He had left the Amish community and worked in our area as a builder for many years. Now he was in his late sixties and no longer able to work alone, doing heavy lifting and putting up drywall, but I knew I could help him. So I asked if he would be interested in taking the renovation job. He offered to do the work for an hourly wage of $20.00, and that was a gift from God.

In every way, God orchestrated the House of Prayer, and the money that we retrieved from the sale of all the catering equipment paid completely for the renovation and furnishings within that made it a wonderful place for prayer.

During the four weeks it took to do the renovation, I held Bible studies and prayer sessions in my home, and we had many pleasant and Spirit-filled times together. I met several very nice and strong Christians. One of them, Don, was a prophet and a watchman on the wall, and God now assigned him as a watchman on the wall for our church. And God gave Don a word for the people.

The Lord had assigned me as a watchman on the wall for the church many years before, but He has, since then, given me different tasks. For one, I was sent to the church to pour out the anointing. When the anointing would leave me and go into others, God would just pour more into me. Praise God!

In time, the House of Prayer became a House of Prayer, Prophecy and Healing, and the place became a springboard for many beginning ministries. I never charged any of the seven different ministries who used that space for their meetings. I even paid the water bills, electric bills and fuel bills and furnished enough chairs to seat forty-five and also the praise and worship music and the flags used in worship and dancing, as well as all of the paper supplies. In this way, God used me to help build other ministries over a three-year period. Today many of these churches have stepped up and opened their own locations to glorify God. In all of this, God showed me how easy it is to build His Church.

After we had been three years in the House of Prayer, God spoke to me and said, "There shall be a gathering of the prophets." The House of Prayer was not to be the location for this gathering. This was to be a traveling ministry within the Tristate area: Maryland, Washington, D.C. and Virginia.

With God, there are seasons and reasons. He puts people in our lives for a season, and we learn from them during that particular season. As we look back throughout the history of the New Testament Church, He did the same with His people then.

Paul's life as a disciple of Christ is a perfect example of this. The many different directions he was sent all had a purpose, and we can glean much from this. People were placed in Paul's life for a certain season and for a certain reason, and then they were removed.

In this way, Paul went from glory to glory, one step at a time. He began as a blind disciple, then became a teacher, a preacher, an evangelist, a prophet and, finally, an apostle. Our tests and trials are what prepares us for the next step in the five-fold ministries.

The Gathering of the Prophets taught me much about prophets and people in the ministry in general—good and bad. For instance, I saw false prophets in operation, people with one foot in the church and the other in the world. They seemed to have dual personalities. My thought, for many of them was, "Chose you today whom you will serve." For my part, I realized that it is important to understand what is being taught. Then, we must take it home and search it out for ourselves to be satisfied that it is really from God.

Through these gatherings, God also taught me much about jealousy in ministry. I learned about gossip and saw backbiters in action. I was able to see things firsthand that sickened me and caused me to withdraw from many of those I had felt close to previously. We are to separate ourselves from those who fail to walk in the ways of the Lord. I thank God for the Holy Spirit, who was teaching me, and I constantly prayed for more discernment.

I was *Maturing in Sonship through Suffering.*

✝ ✝ ✝

How to Worship

Read 1 Chronicles 16:34

O Give thanks unto

The Lord,

For He is good;

And His mercy endures

Forever!

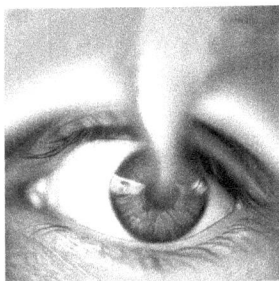

~ NINE ~

A Prophetic Dream

And he dreamed, and behold, a ladder was set up on the earth, and the top of it reached to heaven; and behold, the angels of God were ascending and descending on it. Genesis 28:12

Prophecy can come to us in many ways: in a vision or dream, actually seeing words before our eyes, or receiving a strong impression or conviction. We serve a wonderful God who enjoys and delights in expressing His heart to us in a variety of ways. Jacob received his revelation in a dream.

I have never been one to have a lot of dreams. At least I don't remember many of my dreams. Oh, I had the normal dreams of childhood — running through a field of flowers or feeling some-one was chasing me—but, as an adult, I don't re-member dreaming more than once or twice, and I was unable to remember even those dreams. But then ...

It was six in the morning, and I had just gone to the kitchen to prepare a pot of coffee. The wa-ter was poured in the pot and coffee grounds were placed in the basket, and then, as I reached to turn on the automatic coffeemaker, I heard the Holy Spirit say, "Write your dream!"

Yes, I thought, I did have a dream the night be-fore, but could I even remember it, let alone put it into words? I sat down at the kitchen table and reached for the tablet I saw nearby. I had been working on a Bible study the night before for the next Sunday's class, so I had a pen and pad handy. I quickly began writing down what I could remem-ber of the dream.

Amazingly, as I wrote, the memories of the dream seemed to just roll right out of me onto the paper, as though I were dreaming it live at that very moment. I was not really having to give much thought to what I was writing, and that was un-usual.

When I had finished writing the dream as directed, I went to pour myself a cup of coffee. "Interpret your dream," I then heard the voice say.

Going back to the table (taking a quick sip of coffee on the way), I anxiously began writing the interpretation as it came to me. Again, there was no effort at all being spent on the project. Just so quickly the dream was described, and then just as quickly it was interpreted.

Wow! Pausing to take another good sip of coffee, I began to study what I had just written. First, my description of the vision:

I was standing in the parking lot of a rather large fast-food operation, which had a drive-through window. Then, suddenly, I was inside the restaurant. It was closed and appeared to be under renovation. Chairs were newly painted and sitting throughout the floor space.

I was careful not to rub against those freshly-painted chairs. I can almost remember their smell. Wandering through the restaurant, I noticed a book on the floor and began flipping through the pages of it.

Then, as I continued to stroll through, I came across a large room. There were hundreds of people in the room, and they were all standing. Suddenly, I was at the front of the room and I was teaching from the book I had found.

Next, I saw that I had walked back to the drive-through window. There was an olive-complexioned woman driving the wrong direction through the window. She had a child, a daughter, in the back-seat, buckled into a car seat.

Then I read the interpretation of the dream, as I wrote it that day:

I am called to watch over this operation. "You shall be a watchman on the wall," saith the Lord. "You shall feed the Church."

The food-service operation doesn't surprise me at all. I have been working in the food-service industry since I was fifteen. But I feel the Lord is telling me to open a feeding mission, where souls can be fed with the Word of God.

The chairs being freshly painted are interpreted as old things being gone and all things becoming new. "Their old life shall be gone, and they shall be new creatures, drawing closer to God through salvation." But that is only the beginning, the baby food, if you will.

The book was found on the floor, as if it had received very little respect, almost as if it had been thrown away. As a prophet, I am to take the true Word of God to the lost Church, pulling people out of their comfort zones, teaching and preaching the meat of the Word to a dying Church. "They are hungry; they are thirsty."

The woman was going the wrong way in life, heading in the wrong direction and taking her children with her. "Someone needs to tell the lost what the right direction is." I have been called as an evangelist, especially to women and their families who are going the wrong way in life. They are woman who have been used, abused, misused and cast aside like so much garbage.

In this dream, I have been called to the Church as a preacher, a teacher, a prophet and an evangelist,and not just to one church, but to all churches. My anointing is to be poured out, to overflow onto those churches. What I pour out into them, they will pour out to others, and what I pour out, the Lord will continually resupply.

117

As I look back on this now, I realize that it was a picture of my House of Prayer, Prophecy and Healing. God was giving me an opportunity to help launch other churches, while prophets came out of their shells. The result was that those churches I mentioned previously were launched from that place.

God also showed me how He places people in your life for a particular season. You learn a great deal from them in a short period of time, and then they're gone. You learn the dos and the don'ts, both their honesty and dishonesty. They are there for you to learn from—the good and the bad, and what you learn will mold you into what God wants you to become.

Spiritual gifts are unique endowments from God, given through the Holy Spirit and shared to build up the Body of Christ. Our gifts are given that we may serve others. We are to serve one another with whatever gift each of us has received.

We learn in the New Testament about our spiritual gifts. We have gifts that differ according to the grace given to each of us: prophecy, in proportion to our faith; ministry, in ministering; the teacher, in teaching; the exhorter, in exhortation; the giver, in generosity; the leader, in diligence; the compassionate, in cheerfulness. And it is all done through proclamation, servanthood, teaching the faith, encouragement, generosity, nurturing leadership and extending mercy (as seen in Romans 12:6-8).

Other Spiritual gifts are talked about in 1 Corinthians 12:8-10, 28-30 and Ephesians 4:11, where the five-fold ministry is also mentioned. Primary gifts are those that are surely yours. It is amazing how the Holy Spirit provides for Christian communities, to draw them closer to Himself and help to fulfill His great plan.

At one point, God used Rev. James Powell and his wife, First Lady Johnell Powell, of Christian Family Church in La Plata, Maryland, to help fulfill His plan. Rev. Powell and I had never met, but his name was given to me as one who could and would help. He had a reputation as a giver.

We met, and I asked if I could use his church to open a feeding mission for the homeless and those in need. Within minutes, he began smiling and asked, "When would you like to start?" He not only offered the use of the building, but he also ministered to all those who entered into it. Pastor Powell and his wife are a perfect picture of how

God works through people who are willing vessels for helping others, and in helping others, to do the will of God.

This is a perfect picture of what the Church should be. In every way, I was *Maturing in Sonship through Suffering*.

How to Worship

Read 1 Chronicles 16:29

Give unto the LORD the glory

Due His name.

Bring an offering

And come before Him.

Worship the LORD

In the beauty of holiness!

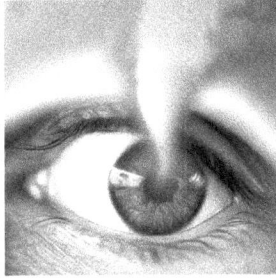

~ TEN ~

"Sit at Her Feet"

Blessed is the man that walketh not in the counsel of the ungodly, nor standeth in the way of sinners, nor sitteth in the seat of the scornful; but his delight is in the law of the LORD, and on His law doth he meditate day and night. And he shall be like a tree planted by the rivers of water that bringeth forth his fruit in his season; his leaf also shall not wither, and whatsoever he doeth shall prosper.

Psalm1:1-3

One day I was drawn to a postcard lying on my kitchen counter. As I came closer to it, I noticed Pastor John Hagee's photo on the front of it. He was to be the special speaker at a Jubilee celebration gathering. "Honey, I called out, "where is Odenton, Maryland?"

"It's near Ft. Meade," he said. "You take 301 to Route 3 toward Baltimore and turn at Route 32 toward Ft. Meade. Odenton is about the third ramp." He paused a moment and then asked, "Why did you want to know?"

I explained that a postcard from the Hagee ministry had come in the mail, and I felt led to go to the meetings they were having. They were going to be at the Full Gospel Emancipation Life Center in Odenton.

"Not so long ago," I told him, "the minister of that church, Dr. Rev. Jackie Norris, was on Juanita Bynam's program, and I was totally mesmerized by her anointing coming through the television. Now I received this postcard, and I feel a strong call to go to her church. It is the beginning of Jubilee, and they are having a four-day revival service." And I went.

I took three guests with me. One of them was a homeless man named Ron. Ron was in need of the Lord. I also took a friend of mine named Fe and her daughter Irene. As the four of us walked down the aisle toward our seat on the third row, center aisle,

Ron turned and looked at me. "Sheila," he said, "I see you preaching in this church."

Strangely enough, I had felt the same thing when I walked through the double doors that led into what they called "the Garden of Eden," and even stronger as we entered into the sanctuary. "I'll claim that!" I replied.

I stood at the entrance to the aisle, letting Irene and Fe go in first, and then leaving a place for Ron beside me (just in case I needed to explain anything to him during the service). For myself, I have always preferred an aisle seat. I like not being closed-in, and I like having space to move about, dance, spread out my arms and worship freely.

After I had noticed the postcard, I immediately went online to the church website. There I saw a photo of the pastor and was sure I would know her if I saw her again. Even though the church began to fill up, I was sure it would not be hard to spot her when she came in. After all, the church was ninety-eight percent African-American, and she was white. (I later learned that it had been her lifelong dream to pastor a black church).

Pastor Jackie was from a small rural town in North Carolina. She grew up on the side of a mountain, looking down on what was called "Shanty Town," a poor, black farming community in a very humble rural setting.

These people were so unlike her current members. At FGELC, a great percentage of the congregation was made up of retired military officers, professionals, and well-educated, beautifully-dressed, loving, caring people. And, oh, how attentive they were to their pastor's every need. You could feel their love from the moment you stepped onto the property.

We were wonderfully welcomed that day. It seemed that everyone who came in came to us and gave us a wonderful love-filled welcome. The presence of God could be felt from the time we entered the parking lot. It was glorious!

The two rows of seats in front of us were reserved for pastors—pastors of that church and visiting pastors as well. As I was not yet an ordained minister at the time, I didn't qualify.

The musicians, a small ensemble of drums, piano, lead and bass guitar and a sax player, began to warm up. What I heard was great. Then, gradually, the singers made their way to the platform, each testing their microphone and motioning either higher or lower to the man in the sound booth.

Bill and I had played around a little with guitars, he on an acoustic guitar and I on the Fender jazz bass. We had always been lovers of music, and I was wishing he was there with me. But his health had been failing for the past few years.

There was another reason Bill was not usually with me. I had gotten Spirit-filled and was operating in the gifts of tongues, prophecy and healings, and the Southern Baptist church he grew up in had always talked against these gifts, saying that they were not for today. Bill was definitely a born-again believer and a wonderful husband, so I didn't press the point. When I had to, I went without him.

The worship began right on time, and everyone jumped to their feet, praising the mighty and awesome name of God. Suddenly the head usher carried two Bibles to the front row and placed them with care and respect. Another usher then led six to eight ministers in, stepping back and directing them with an outstretched hand to the second row.

A few minutes passed, and then the main ministers' entourage came down the aisle, the head usher leading the way. Behind him came Pastor

Jackie's private secretary, followed by Assistant Pastor Barbara Brown (with her husband behind her). Pastor Jackie followed.

I watched as Pastor Brown removed the Bible from his wife's set so that she could sit down, and Barbara removed Pastor Jackie's Bible from her seat for her. Only when Pastor Jackie sat down did the others sit too. There was a perfect order for everything, and I soon learned that this was their way of doing things.

The music now changed to worship, the presence of God was already strong, and I felt that the glory cloud was about to fall. My legs became like rubber, and I stood motionless, with my hands clasped together. The glory of God's presence in that place was so beautiful. It was stronger than I had ever experienced in any church.

For the past few years I had followed Benny Hinn on television and had gone to his crusade's at the Rock Church in Virginia Beach, and also in New York, New Jersey, Pennsylvania and Washington, D.C. The anointing he carried, however, had nothing on this church. What I was feeling that day was just absolutely amazing!

Assistant Pastor Barbara Brown was escorted and assisted up the steps to the platform. She gently placed Minister Jackie's Bible and notes on the podium, opening the Bible to the correct page and making sure the notes were in order.

After Barbara had returned to her seat, the usher escorted Minister Jackie and ushered her up the four stairs to the podium. Everyone was standing as this was done. There was so much honor and respect for this little seventy-some-year-old white lady from the mountains of North Carolina that it was unbelievable. She was a class act! All that we could see was honor and respect, engulfed in perfection, precision and grace.

This was the first evening of their four-day revival or Jubilee Celebration, but I knew immediately that I would be making the drive every evening, for excitement was in the air.

Pastor Jackie asked all the visitors to stand, and we did. She looked at me, and I knew there was a connection of our spirits. It was electric. She asked who we were and where we had come from, and there was a smile and a nod of thank you from her as we replied.

The following evening, as we were leaving the meeting, one of the deacons approached me. "Pastor Jackie would like you to join her and her other ministers for a catered luncheon tomorrow at the Airport Hotel at Baltimore-Washington International Airport," he said. "Would you be able to attend?"

"I would be honored," I answered.

The luncheon was utterly elegant, top-shelf, as was everything these people did.

As I was leaving the luncheon that day, I sat in my car for a moment, reflecting on these events and wondering why I had been the only visitor singled out to join the other fifty for lunch. "Father God, why am I here?" I asked, as tears rolled down my cheeks.

His presence was so strong in my car that the feeling was unexplainable. "You are to sit at her feet for three years!"He told me. Those words continued to echo in my ears and to resonate within me as I drove away: "You are to sit at her feet for three years!"

The following Sunday morning I was at the church again, seated in the same place. During the service I mentioned to Minister Barbara that God had told me I was to sit at the feet of her pastor for the next three years. That next Sunday, as I was leaving, one of the deacons came carrying a rather large box to my car. It was filled with the tape recordings from several years of the pastor's preaching. I knew then what I was to do: I was to listen to her teaching continually, to let the Lord's words in her and through her penetrate my soul. It was wonderful. The anointing of Almighty God was on those tapes.

Writing this reminds me that I must return to listening to them. What a wonderful gift was given to me that day by Pastor Jackie. But, I realized, it was also a gift from God Himself.

On the final night of the Jubilee Celebration, Pastor Jackie stood at the podium and looked at me. "We are going to miss you, Sheila Kay, now that Jubilee is over." She had a way of tilting her head to one side and smiling. That elegant lady, who dressed to the tee, was looking directly at me.

I was inspired to stand and say, "Pastor Jackie, I never said I was going anywhere." She smiled out of the corner of her mouth, and the packed church stood and applauded. It was a wonderful moment!

I attended Pastor Jackie's church, sitting under her anointed ministry, until she went home to be with the Lord. Then I was left with those wonderful anointed tapes. I was *Maturing in Sonship through Suffering.*

✝ ✝ ✝

How to Worship

Read 1 Chronicles 16:25-26

For Great is the LORD

And greatly to be praised.

He is also to be feared above all gods.

For all the gods of the people are idols,

But the LORD

(the Creator of All Things)

Made the heavens!

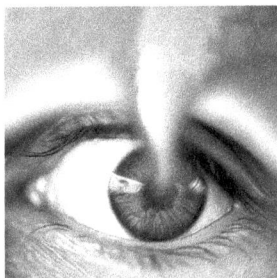

~ ELEVEN ~

"Sit Next to Claire on the Plane"

And the Lord shall guide thee continually.

Isaiah 58:11

As I boarded the El Al plane for Israel, I was amazed at the width of the fuselage and the overall massive size of the aircraft. Both the right and left sides of the plane had three seats in each row, while the center section had six seats to each row. There was a special place along the wall for the Jewish rabbis to pray, as they covered themselves in their prayer shawls (the *tallit*) and rocked back and forth in communion with God.

The plane had a wide spiral staircase going to the upper deck. While walking down the aisle toward the back of the plane, I kept asking the women who were sitting alone, "Is your name Claire or Claria?" All of them shook their heads in the negative. I was sure the Lord had told me to sit next to someone named Claire or Claira.

When I couldn't find anyone by that name, I ended up next to a woman from India who was now living in New Jersey. She was very pleasant, and we spent a lot of time talking during the flight. I never did run into a Claire or a Claria during the whole trip. Perhaps I had heard the Lord wrong when He said, "Sit next to Claire on the plane."

Visiting Israel was a wonderful experience. I was amazed at the way time had seemed to stand still in many areas of the country. Shepherds could be seen on the hillsides wearing the same type of garb men like them wore thousands of years before.

I had been led to go with the Benny Hinn tour, and we had nightly services on the shores of the Sea of Galilee and a water baptism in the Jordan River. We swam in the Dead Sea and visited all the places made famous because Jesus had done something there. All the while, I searched for Claire.

It was all delightful, but I got the most emotional at a church in the old part of Jerusalem. Tears streamed down my face, and the anointing was so strong on me that one of the nuns in that place stared at me as I worshiped. I was sure that my face must be shining with the glory of God.

On the return trip home, I sat in the front row. There were three seats in that row, and I was in the middle seat. A woman to my left was from India, and an elderly man sat to my right. He had gone to Israel to attend the funeral of his business partner. Together they had a tool and dye business in Rochester, New York.

I could tell that he was Jewish, and he was able to tell me quite a lot about the Goldbergs and the part of Germany they had lived in. I took advantage of the opportunity and, for at least four hours, talked to him about Jesus and the spiritual revelations I had been experiencing since being filled with the Holy Spirit. He was amazed.

The reason this man had been seated in the front row was that he needed a wheelchair. He could transfer from his chair to a seat in the airplane more easily at the front. Then his chair was stored out of sight.

I asked him when he planned to return to Israel, and he said this was to be his last trip. I sensed at that moment that he was terminally ill and asked if I could pray for him. He said, "Yes."

"What is your name?" I asked.

"Morton Clariton," was his reply.

So that was it! God had placed me in that seat to witness to Mr. Clariton. I had understood it as Claira or Claire.

It was only when the plane landed in New York that I began explaining to him the revelation God had given about Claira and was wishing I had done it sooner. If I had explained the revelation before I knew his name, it might have had more impact on him. I watched from the window as Morton was wheeled to a limo on the tarmac and driven away. What an interesting man! What a fantastic trip! And what a fascinating God we serve!

If you are ever not certain you have understood the Lord, ask Him to repeat what He has said. You may have heard it wrong. I planted the seed, and God will water it.

I was *Maturing in Sonship through Suffering.*

How to Worship

Read 1 Chronicles 16:7-8

Give thanks constantly.

Call upon His name.

Witness to others

About His greatness.

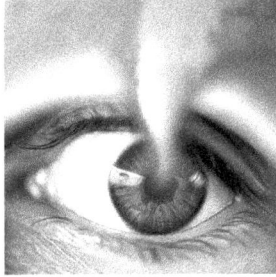

~ TWELVE ~

Jail and Street Ministry

Go out into the highways and hedges and compel
them to come in, that my house may be filled.

Luke 14:23

I was employed for a time with a food contract service that managed jails, prisons and correction centers throughout Maryland. Because of doing this, we had direct contact with the inmates, who worked in various positions in the kitchen. This gave us the opportunity to talk with them and witness to them on an ongoing basis. This was so wonderful that I was saddened when we eventually lost that contract.

Then, however, special Christian training courses within the jail made room for workforce devel-

139

opment training for inmates in the special programs, and I was asked to teach these programs. The program helped inmates to become certified in food service, and this would give them greater employment opportunities when they were eventually released.

There are many Christian volunteers within our prison systems. They teach parenting skills, English writing and reading skills, dog interaction, Bible studies, Spanish classes and much more. I was amazed at the number of Christians who were reaching out in this way to inmates, and they, too, use the classes as a way to testify of Jesus.

I was approached by a Stephen Minister [2] from a local Lutheran Church about becoming a Minister and Leader of that program. The training was for assisted living, working with the elderly, prison aftercare, or wherever heartfelt care was needed. I agreed to take part.

I worked for several months in aftercare, just to get a feel of it, but the Lord showed me this was

---

2. "Stephen Ministry is the one-to-one lay caring ministry that takes place in congregations that use the Stephen Series system. Stephen Ministry congregations equip and empower lay caregivers—called Stephen Ministers—to provide high-quality, confidential, Christ-centered care to people who are hurting." From https://www.stephenministries.org

just part of the testing ground for me. He was developing me for other adventures where this program could also be used.

As a watchman on the wall for the Church, I was never certain where the Lord would send me on Saturdays or Sundays. I got my clothes ready for those days, and then He would tell me where I was to go. It was all about just allowing His anointing to flow through me. How exciting! I was *Maturing in Sonship through Suffering.*

✝✝✝

I'm in a

Desperate Way

For More of God!

Hear me, Oh Lord,

I need You!

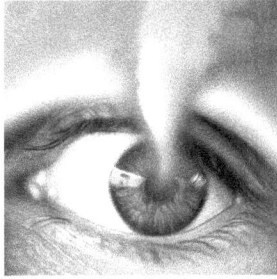

~ THIRTEEN~

"In the Body or Out," I Do Not Know

And I knew such a man (whether in the body or out of the body I cannot tell — God knoweth).
2 Corinthians 12:3

One night, after turning out all the lights and locking the doors, I went to my bedroom to get ready for bed. I opened a dresser draw and removed my pajamas, laying them on the bed. My Bible was lying there, and I felt compelled to pick it up, and I began reading.

Immediately, whether in the body or out, I do not know, I was standing on the sidewalk in Southeast Washington, D.C., at the corner of Martin Luther King and Malcolm X Avenues.

Since I grew up in Southeast D.C., I was very familiar with this lower-income ghetto-type community. It was an area of drug users, alcoholics, the undereducated and the unemployed. This is the area where I teach job skills to those who are in need of employment. I worked through the Petty Greene Center, across from St. Elizabeth's Mental Hospital, and also from the United Planning Organization on Good Hope Road in Anacostia. So I knew this area well.

The particular area where I now found myself standing had a view looking down on Bolling Air Force Base, the Anacostia River, the Washington Monument and the landscape of Alexandria, Virginia and the District of Columbia.

Across from where I stood were hundreds of African-American men. Many of them had their sons with them, teenage and younger. They were all dressed for combat, and their attitude was of militant, jail-house Muslims. All of the men had automatic weapons resting across their arms, and most of the teenagers were armed as well. There were so many that it was difficult to get a count, but my estimate was that there were somewhere around five to six hundred.

I called out to one of the men I recognized, but he just looked at me, saying nothing. I shouted out, "Where are you going? What are you doing?" Again there was no answer. I cried out once more, "Where are you going? What are you doing?"

This time, without making eye contact, one of the men spoke. He said, "We're headed for the Capital and White House. We're taking over."

Even as he was speaking, the men began moving out down the hill toward the Southeast Freeway that would lead to the South Capitol Street Bridge, and that would leave them less than a mile from the Capital of the United States of America. From the Capital going west, it would be just one mile to the Washington Monument, which sits in the backyard of the White House. Immediately I was back on the edge of my bed with the Bible in my hands, and I was weeping.

Six months after this, I was driving from Waldorf to Fredericksburg, Virginia, with a husband-and-wife couple (Mr. and Mrs. Song), who were going with me to the Living Word Fellowship with hosts, Pastors Richard and Christine Dunk. I had become a member of Gospel Crusade Ministerial Fellowship out of Stevens, Pennsylvania, and Pastor Richard is the East Coast Regional Director of that organization. We were having a gathering of all the churches under his guidance, and represented would be ministers from Florida to Maine. As we drove the one-hour trip to the church in Virginia, I was telling the Songs about the out-of-body experience I'd had and what the Lord had showed me.

The service began with praise and then went into worship, and I noticed a female pastor who approached the altar and knelt down. After about five minutes, she stood and began weeping, as she started giving a testimony to what God had just shown her. Amazingly, her testimony was the same thing I had seen in my out-of-body experience, with the exception that she didn't know the street names or locations, for she was from Florida.

When she finished, I stood and gave my testimony and had Mr. and Mrs. Song testify to what I had told them on our trip to Fredericksburg of my out-of-body experience.

When we broke for lunch that day, this was the talk of the conference. This revelation entrusted to us was important enough that God wanted it released to those many people during the conference, and it is something we all must pray against.

Whether in the body or out of the body, I do not know, but what I do know is that this was real! I am certain that this same revelation has been given to many others in the Christian community at large.

The Lord had placed me at that one location, one that I was most familiar with, and I saw what was happening there. But He also showed me that others were marching at the same time as the men I saw. They were looking at their watches, synchronizing the time, as they began moving down East Capitol Street, North Capitol Street, Southern Avenue, Pennsylvania Avenue, M Street—all leading to the U.S. Capital and the White House. And God continues to tell me, "This experience must be told, and it must be prayed against, to defeat the evil one."

I was *Maturing in Sonship through Suffering.*

✝✝✝

Music in Church

Is to prepare

The heart,

Not to entertain!

It is:

Prayer, praise, passion,

prophecy, preparation, and

participation

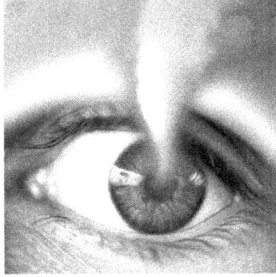

"Choose You This Day Whom Ye Will Serve"

Choose you this day whom ye will serve.

Joshua 24:15

I awoke lying in a puddle of blood at the foot of the steps that led to our second-floor landing. Two of my daughters shared a room at the top right rear, and my youngest daughter was in the crib in our master bedroom, located to the right front. I was shivering from shock and cold, and every bone in my body ached. I reached for a throw rug that lay by the door beside me and tossed it over me. I was afraid to stand, afraid that the baby I was carrying had died and might come out.

My husband had come home drunk again and when I asked about the lipstick on his shirt collar, he had sucker-punched me in the stomach, and I had fallen down the steps. He hadn't gotten home until around 3 a.m., and the bars had all closed at 2, so I knew he was up to his usual no-good.

He was now moving around upstairs, so I knew it must be 7 a.m., and he was getting ready to open the gas station my dad had bought for us. Dad had done so much for us—purchasing our first car, arranging for the purchase of the Exxon Station to support us and even making the deposit on our row house on Elmira Street in Southwest Washington.

When we had married, I was just fifteen. My husband was seventeen and had tried to join the military, but because he had asthma, he was rejected. He did serve in the National Guard and there he attended mechanics school, where he learned to fix cars and trucks. In this way, he became one of the leading mechanics in the Ft. Washington area.

He was coming down the steps now, and I pretended to be asleep. Without a word, he stepped over me, as if I wasn't even there at all, and exited out through the kitchen to the back door. My body was blocking the front door.

I had been lying there now for four hours, and I didn't want to get up until he left. I was nineteen years old, had three children and was in my third month of pregnancy with my fourth. My children were my life.

As for my husband, I had come to hate him. Verbal and physical abuse were his way of life, so the children were the only wonderful thing I had left. In truth, I was a child myself growing up with my own children.

His father did all of our grocery shopping, as he had always done for his own wife, and I was not allowed to have any money at all for any purpose. Everything was strictly controlled. I had once asked for chocolate milk for the children and been denied. He called it "a waste of money."

One excuse after another had been conjured up for my parents and in-laws about the frequent bruises I bore. In the back of their minds, they must have known that I was being abused. They had to know. I lived in constant fear and had to learn just to keep my mouth shut to avoid the consequences.

My joy was taking the kids for walks or going with them to the playground at the top of Elmira Street. When my husband failed to come home on many occasions, I would borrow milk from the neighbors, just enough for cereal or baby bottles. Looking back on it now, I thank God for our neighbor Mrs. Chaconeus. Since we lived in row houses, I'm certain the entire neighborhood must have heard me bouncing off the walls at one time or another.

Medical insurance was not available in the 1950s, so we had to pay out of pocket when we went to the doctor or hospital. So, we mostly just didn't go. I didn't go that day either. Instead, after my husband left for work that morning in early November, I pulled myself up by the door knob and walked slowly up the stairs to the bathroom. The bleeding had stopped, and I cleaned myself up and lay on the couch most of the day, where I could watch the children. Terry, my youngest, stayed in the stroller. I wouldn't be picking her up much that day, only to change her.

Something was different now in me and in our marriage. A part of me had died. I didn't care if my husband ever came home or not. It no longer mattered. It was over. Something had died; our marriage itself was dead.

Divorce was unheard of back then, and there were no shelters for abused women or children.

You just had to take the abuse. Many women died at the hands of their husbands, and, for the most part, it was all conveniently swept under the rug.

During my eighth month of pregnancy, labor pains began. Dad and Mom came and took me to the hospital, where my first son was born. Strangely, I named him after his father.

He was a beautiful baby, but there were serious complications. He had been born with only one quarter of a brain and was never able to leave the hospital. I would visit and look at him through the window of the nursery. I remember it as though it were yesterday. My beautiful baby lived for only four weeks, and then he died.

We had no money for a funeral, so my baby was cremated and his ashes spread on the ground with other unclaimed bodies at the D.C. Morgue. That was the picture that filled my mind for years, and the rest of me died that day.

Mrs. Chaconeus had given me a beautiful baby-blue sweater set with a hat and little blue socks to match. Now, that was all I had of my son. I was devastated. Then something unusual happened.

A friend of my husband had been the town drunk for many years. People called him Bucket

Head. He was a hopeless alcoholic who'd had DTs[3] so bad he was put in a mental hospital. But, lo and behold, when he came out of there, he was a new man. Everyone said he had become a religious fanatic and had gone from one extreme to another.

The evening of my son's death this man stood at our door. Looking at my husband, he said, "I want you and Sheila to come with me and my wife."

My husband loved this man like a father, but he was skeptical and asked, "Where are we going?"

"Just come on," his friend said. "You'll know when we get there."

I was nearly non-responsive at that point. I didn't care where I went. I was numb with grief.

Bucket Head took us to a Baptist church in Marlow Heights, and they were having a revival. "What's a revival?" I was thinking.

The preacher preached that night, and every word he said was meant for me. I didn't know what this was all about, but I knew that God was talking directly to me.

Then music began to play, and the choir began to sing. The words they sang were so powerful:

---

3. Not as well known now as in that time, DTs refers to *Delirium Tremens*, the symptoms associated with alcohol withdrawal.

Softly and tenderly Jesus is calling,
  Calling for you and for me;
See on the portals He's waiting and watching,
  Watching for you and for me!

Come home! Come home!
  Ye who are weary, come home!
Earnestly, tenderly, Jesus is calling,
  Calling, O sinner, come home! [4]

Tears began to roll down my cheeks, and I lifted myself out of my outside aisle seat to go forward. Immediately my husband grabbed my arm and yanked me back into my seat. "Don't you dare embarrass me in front of these people," he said. I laughed to myself because he didn't know any of those people.

Bucket Head grabbed his arm and said, "Let her go! Let her go!"

My husband released me, and I made my way to the front of the church, where I was convinced God had called me to go. I was coming home. God had called me and then had refused to allow my husband to hold me back.

---

4. Words and music by Will Lamertine Thompson (1847-1909)

Women from the church came to the front of the altar and ministered to me. They held me and loved on me. I didn't have a clue what was happening, but I knew it was something beautiful. A peace had come over me, a peace I had never felt before.

A few days later, the women evangelists who had prayed with me at the altar came to our home to minister to me some more, but my husband refused to let them in. He told them to go away and never come back. I cried the rest of the day.

The next morning, after my husband had left for work, I packed my children up and asked my mother to watch them while I went out to find a job and a place to move. I had to leave this man. He was bad news and getting worse.

This should have signaled a wonderful new beginning for me, but just the opposite happened. Alone and afraid, and wondering how in the world I would be able to support my children, I began a dizzying downward spiral into sin.

Before long, I was frequenting the barrooms myself and doing things I would never have imagined myself doing. I was never able to rent anything more than one room for us, and I couldn't afford a babysitter to stay with my children while I worked. Thank God for grandmothers. First, they stayed with my parents and then with my mother-in-law.

The death of my son was just eating me up inside. There is no greater loss on earth than to lose a child, and it doesn't matter what age they are. That child is bone of your bone and flesh of your flesh. Children are gifts from God, and they need to be loved and nurtured, not abused and hurt.

And death is so final, so empty and so unchangeable. The death of this child seemed even worse for me, because there was no grave to mourn over, no place to kneel and pray, or to leave a flower or a note. I was grief stricken and inconsolable.

I had never gone back to church, but I had bought myself a Bible called *The Word*. It seemed easier for me to understand than the King James Version, and I read it. I read it when I was drunk, and I read it when I was sober. I had a hunger that needed to be fed somehow. Looking back now, I realize that I would never have made it through those alcoholic years without the Word.

Then came a worse blow. I had lost my son, and now I was about to lose my daughters as well. At first, they had stayed with my in-laws, but then they had to move. The house they were renting was sold, and they were unable to find anything suitable nearby. So they moved out of the area altogether.

My husband sold our house and the business and moved away too. (In the process, he forged my name on every legal document, so I had no say in any of it.) Now, I was about to lose my other three children through the courts, as if I hadn't been devastated enough already.

Three years after we had separated, my husband filed for divorce. I hired a lawyer from Baltimore to defend me. He was a friend and said he wouldn't charge anything. I sent him all the necessary papers, but when the time came for me to appear in court, he didn't let me know about it. The result was that the divorce proceeded without me, and I lost custody of my children.

This inspired another downward spiral in my life and was just another excuse to drink. I blamed myself for not staying with my husband and taking the abuse. I also blamed myself for walking away from him. I blamed myself for everything. I was a worthless failure. I had failed myself and my children.

One evening, I was watching Evangelist Billy Graham on television, and I responded to his altar call and rededicated my life to the Lord. This time I sought out a church home.

The only church I was familiar with was the Baptist, so I began attending a Baptist church. I was still very immature in my faith, and I had one foot in the church and the other in the world. But I continued to grow and drank less and less.

Then one day the Lord suddenly took it all away: the drinking, the smoking, the night life. Change came one stepping stone at a time. I had become a new creature in Christ Jesus, but now I had to choose whom I would serve.

I was twenty years old when I finally accepted the Lord as my Savior, and I remained in the wilderness for a very long time, just trying to get it right. During that time, I remarried and had two more children. My oldest daughter from my first marriage, who was now fifteen, ran away from her father and came to live with me.

It took me forty years from the day of my salvation before I was filled with the Holy Spirit with the evidence of speaking in tongues. From then on, I have walked in a heavy anointing, surrendered to My Lord for any purpose He has for me. It was a life-changing experience in every way.

My latest commission from the Lord has been to go to the Church, as a watchman on the wall, for God's people must prepare themselves for His coming by implementing the five-fold ministry.

Revival is coming, and the evangelist, the teacher, the pastor, the prophet and the apostle must all be prepared to handle the influx of people who will be coming to the Lord in the days ahead.

The Lord is showing us how we must walk, according to Galatians 4:1:

- Walk in the Holy Spirit.
- Walk in the vocation you have been called to (the greatest calling of all is to salvation).
- Walk in lowliness and meekness with long-suffering and love.
- Keep the unity of the Spirit in the bond of peace.
- Keep your focus on the one Body, one Spirit, one hope of your calling, one God and Father of all, through all and in all.

- Your gift is for the perfecting of the saints.
- It is for the building up the Body of Christ.
- It is to bring all into the unity of the faith and the knowledge of the Son of God.
- Do not be tossed to and fro by every false doctrine, where they lie in wait to deceive.
- Walk in your calling and perfect it.

I had made my choice of who to serve, and I was not looking back. Rather, I was *Maturing in Sonship through Suffering.*

✝✝✝

How to Worship

Read Isaiah 1:16-17

Wash you,

Make you clean.

Put away the evil of your doings

From before My eyes.

Cease to do evil

(sin defiles,

And then you have a need

For a spiritual "washing.")

Learn to do well.

Seek judgment.

Relieve the oppressed.

Judge the fatherless.

Plead for the widow!

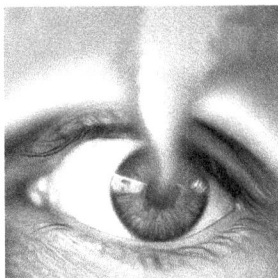

~ FIFTEEN ~

"I Am the Lord that Healeth Thee"

If thou wilt diligently hearken to the voice of the LORD thy God, and wilt do that which is right in His sight, and wilt give ear to His commandments and keep all His statutes, I will put none of these diseases upon thee which I have brought upon the Egyptians; for I am the LORD that healeth thee.

Exodus 15:26

Through the years, God saw fit to give me additional side businesses. As I have noted, I had always worked in food service, but I was also given many other talents that helped to support me and my children and left us beholden to no man.

165

My sister Jean was much more like my mother. She loved to sleep late in the morning, while I was an early riser like Dad. He and I would have breakfast together on the weekends, and afterwards he would read the paper, and I would polish his shoes for the upcoming work week.

Whenever he did any type of construction in our home, I was the one who helped him. Whether it was laying tile, working with drywall, doing plumbing or carpentry, I was always at his side. I was his daughter, yet I was also the son he never had. It was a lasting bond, and these were lessons that followed me my whole life.

I started a cleaning service that worked with construction companies doing pre-occupancy clean-up of their new homes. This soon led to cleaning commercial kitchens for Bob's Big Boy Restaurants and other commercial sites. In this work, I spent much time climbing ladders, stooping, bending and scrubbing. Through many years of this, my knees took a beating, and I ended up with torn ligaments on the outside of the knee and a torn meniscus on the inside of the knee. I went to an orthopedic doctor who specialized in sports medicine. He told me I would need surgery, but the voice inside me said no.

In time, however, going up and down stairs became very painful for me, and I could no longer do the daily tasks of the job and was forced to close my cleaning service. I began praying over my left knee for complete healing:

> *"Father, You said in Your Word that You are the God that heals. [5] I believe Your Word, Father. You are not a man that You should lie. "You also said it is Your will that I should prosper and be in health. [6] Again, Father, You are not a man that You should lie. You said it, Father, and I believe it. You said it, and I believe every word You have spoken. I wait for my healing, Father, in the name of Jesus."*

After that, I didn't give it another thought, but within a few days, my knee was completely healed and has never pained me again. I give all honor and glory to the Lord for my healing. He is truly the God that heals.

5. This prayer was based on the promise of Exodus 15:26.
6. This prayer was based on the promise of 3 John 2.

One evening I went to bed, and no sooner had I lain down than pain surged through my back. The next morning the pain was still there. I called my lady doctor and made an appointment to have it checked out.

Dr. G scheduled me for an MRI, and the lab was able to work me in that same day. The next day I picked up the disk and paper work that described my problem and dropped it off at the doctor's office. She called and asked me to come in immediately. When I got there, she said, "You have gallstones, Sheila," and she handed me a card with a surgeon's name on it and said I should contact him as soon as possible.

"Doc," I said, "you know me better than that. I have all my major body parts and have no intention of having surgery to have them removed ... unless it's totally necessary."

I went home and pulled down a book on nutritional healing from the shelf and flipped the pages to gall bladder and then gallstones to see what they recommended. I was amazed when I saw how simple their suggested solution was. "I'll give this a try first," I decided. "If it doesn't work, then I'll go back to the doctor."

The directions read:

Mix 2 tablespoons of extra virgin olive oil and the juice of ½ fresh lemon. Take this mixture prior to going to bed at night and again in the morning upon awakening. Do this for 3 days. On the morning of the 3rd day, follow it with pure (not from concentrate) simple apple juice.

I did that, and it worked, and I never had that pain again.

Father, I praise Your holy name. I give You all the praise, the honor and the glory, for You are the God that healeth me.

I was *Maturing in Sonship through Suffering*.

✝ ✝ ✝

How to Worship

Read Isaiah 1:18

Come now,

Let us reason together,

Says the Lord.

Though your sins be as scarlet,

They shall be white as snow.

Though they be red like crimson,

They shall be as wool....

(This can only be accomplished

Through faith in Christ

And His shed blood.)

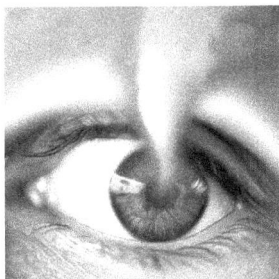

~ Sixteen ~

A Christmas Gift from God

But not as the offense, so also is the free gift.
Romans 5:15

We were preparing for a special meeting at my home in Waldorf. Our goal was to bring together a select group from the Christian community to assist with housing, food, clothing and gifts for the homeless and their children. A realtor friend of mine named Gail and Exit Real Estate Company in White Plains, Maryland were heading up the project, and already we had several families housed in local motels until more permanent housing could become available.

I was invited to a Christmas holiday dinner and play at the Baptist Church of St. Charles, and there was a full house. God orchestrated my seating, as usual. This was the church Bill and I had attended for many years and where he was a deacon. I was a member there when I became filled with the Holy Spirit. It was the same church where I had taught the Bible class, the same church where, as I was teaching my first Vacation Bible School class, small children had begun to weep, and I took two of them to the pastor to talk with him about their salvation.

This was the same church where I was in a Sunday evening Bible Study class when blood began to drip from the cross, the same church I was in when the Holy Spirit told me to go to another town and lay hands on a man with prostate cancer. Now, as I sat at a round table, talking with friends, both old and new, I was asked. "Where do you work, Sheila?"

I didn't know the woman who had asked this, but she had overheard me speak of food sanitation. "I'm self-employed, I answered, "but I work in Work-Force Development, with the inner-city at-risk youth and jail population."

"What type of jobs are developed?" she asked.

"I train people in food-service sanitation and management, and I do these classes throughout D.C., Maryland and Virginia," I answered.

A big smile came across her face, and she said, "I run the H.R. Department for one of the largest food-service companies on the East Coast and have hundreds of jobs coming available over the next five months that I can dedicate to this type of project. Please give me your information."

"And here is my business card," she added.

Praise God! I wanted to jump up out of my seat and run the room in Pentecostal style, but I contained myself. You can be sure I was running on the inside.

I urge you to turn your life over to God, for only He knows the beginning from the end. He has designed and will orchestrate your life. Surrender it to Him completely, and you'll be amazed at what He will do with it.

Thank You, Father, for all You do for me. I will love You and worship You forever. Amen!

I was *Maturing in Sonship through Suffering.*

✝ ✝ ✝

The past will always reoccur

until we change our thinking!

Read Proverbs 23:7

Commit your work

Unto the LORD,

And your thoughts

Will be established.

Destiny (Romans 5:4)

Character (Romans 5:4)

Habits (Psalm 11:7)

Action (James1:24)

Thoughts (2 Corinthians 10:15)

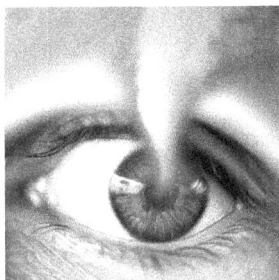

Leading More Men and Women to Christ

Come unto Me all ye that labor and are heavy laden, and I will give you rest. Take My yoke upon you and learn of Me, for I am meek and lowly in heart, and ye shall find rest unto your souls.

Matthew 11:28-29

I had taken over our church's pantry committee and was not very happy about either the guidelines of the operation or the policies and procedures involved. I guess my thought was, "If you're hungry today, then more than likely you'll be hungry tomorrow or the next day." Still, we were only allowed to feed any given family once a month.

179

Secondly, to receive our aid, they had to show a driver's license or have proof of where they lived. And, if they were not from the immediate area, they were not allowed to get any food at all. That troubled me.

Yes, there were some people who went around from church to church getting food from numerous churches and selling it to get drugs, but that should not hinder us from giving to deserving families. The truth is that it's hard to determine where a real need lies, and that's very sad.

My purpose in taking this position had been to use the opportunity to witness to the individuals or families who came for help. It didn't matter to me what their physical need was; I realized that their greatest need was to have Jesus in their lives.

Meeting me and seeing the attitude with which I handled their situation might be the only glimpse they got of God that day. I wanted to put forth an attitude of love, letting them know that I and the church I represented truly cared about them and their families, and we were ready to do whatever was necessary to help them.

One particular day I met Lee, a very attractive woman in her mid-forties. Her hair, clothing and make-up were meticulous, and yet she had a street-smart way about her.

I learned a lot about Lee in a short period of time. There was a hunger in her, and I tapped into that hunger. I saw through many of the things she said, and I met her at the point of her real need.

Lee had been raised in the Catholic Church and educated in a Catholic school, but she had never been told about the plan of salvation. She didn't know Jesus as her Savior, and she knew nothing about the love the Father had for her.

When I caught sight of her desire, it opened a door for me to teach her. "Lee," I said, "would you like to come to my home for Bible study once a week?"

"How many people come?" she asked.

"Just you," was my response. She loved it.

The following Monday at 7 p.m. we began our first study in the Word. "Bible 101" is what I called the class. We began with the book of John and covered the basics.

Lee had many questions, and from that point forward she called me daily, often several times a day, always to ask a spiritual question or to talk about Jesus. "I want what you have, Sheila," she said. "I want to know the Bible the way you do, and I want to know Jesus like you do."

She would often say, "I just love to hear you talk about Jesus," and it was true. She really did.

Lee had a horrible childhood, one that sent her into a life of drugs, alcohol, sex, beatings and addiction to pain killers. She had been physically hurt in many ways—through beatings, falls and accidents. In her mind, this was her reason for taking drugs, but I felt in my heart that the drugs were more of a way for her to escape the pain and the hurts of life, more than her physical pain.

She had been molested by her father from an early age, as had her sister Joan. The two of them would always refer to him as "Buzzard." It was only a matter of weeks before Lee asked if Joan could join the Bible studies. At the beginning, Joan was distracting to me. She needed far too many cigarette breaks. But I knew that God would take care of that habit one day.

In their family, there had been seven sisters and seven brothers. The boys had all been sent away to Boys Town, Father Flanagan's famous Catholic home for boys in Omaha, Nebraska. The sisters had stayed at home and suffered it out. They would tell me how their mother had to flee to keep "Buzzard" from beating or even killing her. She would have to run down dark country roads and hide in ditches half-filled with filthy water, as he chased her with a gun during his drunken rages.

Later, Lee told me, their family doctor began having sex with her. In exchange, he gave her drugs. From an early age, she learned how to manipulate men, and they knew how to manipulate her. This became, for her, a way of life.

Although the girls had all attended Catholic school, they had never received Jesus as personal Savior. They had never read the Bible and had never been taught to pray from the heart, while building a closer relationship with God. They had no idea how tangible the Holy Spirit is or how He can live in us and work through us.

Lee had a daughter, who had also lived a life of Hell, simply because her mother was addicted to everything you could think of. This daughter, whom I will call Candy, was what is commonly called a "cutter." [7] She had marks up and down

7. The Urban Dictionary defines *cutter* as: "One who cuts themselves to relieve themselves from an emotional pain." This "can be done," the dictionary states, "with any sharp object, such as, but not limited to, knives, razors, broken glass, broken CD's, scissors,

her arms where she would cut herself with razor blades. Other than that, Candy was a beautiful girl.

Joan had a twin sister whom Buzzard shot and killed at their kitchen table during one of his drunken stupors. They had all lied for him, but he had done a brief stint in prison anyway. As head of the household, he was needed at home, officials reasoned, so he was released.

Another of the sisters had killed herself. I cannot even imagine the terrible life these girls lived. What they suffered seemed beyond belief, even though I knew it was all true.

Lee's hunger continued to grow. I opened the Bible one evening and led her down what is known among evangelical Christians as The Roman Road, or the Roman Road to Salvation. [8] This method of studying the plan of salvation uses passages from the book of Romans to outline God's promises and commands.

As we studied the Roman Road, I had Lee read each passage, and then I asked her what that pas-

and safety pins." From http://www.urbandictionary.com/define.php?term=cutter.

8. "The Roman Road to Salvation is a selection of Bible verses taken from the book of Romans that present the plan of salvation through faith in Jesus Christ." From https://www.teenmissions.org/resources/roman-road-to-salvation/.

sage said to her. We talked over her answers, and then we continued down the Road. She knew these truths in her heart, she believed what she was reading, and as she came to understand it, she was born again. I could see her life changing.

Lee was not only growing; she was now glowing with the glory of the Lord. The hunger and thirst she displayed can only come from Him.

One Saturday Lee and I went to church together, and then we went to dinner, all the while talking about Jesus. I could never get enough of Him, and neither could she.

Afterward, when we pulled into the parking lot of the apartment complex where Lee lived. She thanked me for dinner and for taking her to church. "Sheila, I want what you have," she said again. "I don't know exactly what it is, but I want it."

At that moment, the Holy Spirit directed me to lay hands on her. "Father," I prayed, "fill Lee with the Holy Spirit. Give her, Lord, what You have given me. Fill her, Father.'"

I then quoted Peter in Acts 3:6, *"Silver and gold have I none, but such as I have give I thee."*

"Fill her, Lord God, fill her," I continued to pray. "Amen, amen, and amen!"

At that moment, I felt a transfer of power, and I began to tremble. "Oh my God, what is that wonderful feeling, Sheila?" Lee asked. "What is happening? Oh my God, what is happening? It is wonderful! Sheila, what is happening?"

Her response was almost unbelievable. She was experiencing an infilling of the Holy Spirit, and it was beautiful to see.

"Thank You Lord! Thank You, Lord!" I said.

And I heard Lee echo, "Yes, thank You, Lord!"

I went on home, and Lee called me about an hour later. "Sheila," she said, "I still have that feeling. It's beyond belief. What is it? What is happening?"

"That, my friend, is the presence of Almighty God," I told her. "You are being filled with His glorious presence. The Holy Spirit has taken up residence within you. Enjoy it and thank Him.

"And, Lee, now is the time to ask for healing. Now is the time to ask for your daughter's salvation. Now is the time to ask God to release and deliver you from bondage. And love on Him. He loves you so much!"

For the next three days Lee was overwhelmed with God's presence and, over the next few weeks and months, her focus left herself and was now concentrated on her daughter. She wanted her daughter to be saved.

But Candy was very uncomfortable around me. She was under conviction and avoided me at every turn. Satan had his claws firmly in her.

Over the next two years it was amazing to see how Lee grew in Christ. Even though I knew that she was occasionally taking too many pain pills, it was hard for me to point out to her, for she'd had back surgery several times and also neck surgery. I could not judge the constant pain she walked in. Her injuries had come, not only from beatings suffered at the hands of her father, but also her husband and her boyfriends. Having been abused her whole life, it was what she expected, and I could identify with that because of what I had suffered with my first husband.

I learned that Pastor Benny Hinn was going to be in Baltimore, and I invited Lee to go with me to the meetings. Because of all the walking we would have to do, I asked if we should bring a wheelchair, and she agreed.

I had volunteered to work at the book tables, so an usher placed Lee in the wheelchair section. Every now and then I would go and check on her. By the time the meeting had started, she had met two men who were also in wheelchairs and had come for a healing touch from Pastor Benny.

Once the music started, I went in and sat near Lee. I could tell immediately that she was over-dosed on some sort of medication. Her speech was slurred, and she wasn't acting normal.

"Lee, what drugs did you take?" I asked.

As it turned out, one of the men she had met had given her some sort of pain killer. It's amazing how people who have a drug problem are drawn to one another like magnets. She took the pills and didn't have a clue what she was taking.

On the ride home, which was the longest hour and a half I had ever spent, Lee kept looking for her purse, although she was holding it in her lap. I told her this, but she didn't think that was a purse. She thought it was a dog.

Then she couldn't seem to find her key. It, too, was in her hand. She was just totally out of it.

When we arrived at her apartment, I told her I would call her in the morning and pick her up at 9 a.m. to go back for day two of the conference. I called as I had promised, but Lee didn't answer her phone. "I'll just let her sleep," I decided.

When I returned from the conference that evening, I called Lee again, but she didn't seem to be home.

The following day I called her again, and again I got no answer. Worried now, I went to the apartment complex and asked a maintenance man to open the apartment door for me. As I had feared, Lee's body was found on the kitchen floor. She was dead. She had put her nightgown on when she got home from Baltimore, but her bed had not been slept in. She had gone to the kitchen to get a drink to take some more medications. An autopsy revealed that her throat muscles had been so relaxed from the drugs she had taken earlier that she could not swallow and had choked to death with the pills and water still in her throat.

Lee's funeral was very sad. I was there to comfort Joan, who was very childlike. She came over to where I was sitting, put her head on my shoulder, and began to weep.

The service was held at New Life Church in La Plata, but her burial was at the Catholic cemetery where she had attended school. There was a family plot there, and a Catholic priest was in charge of her internment.

He approached me and said, "I understand you were a friend of Lee's and were there for her. Thank you for that." He may have thought he was now bringing Lee home to God, but I knew that the moment she had breathed her last, she had awoken in His presence. She was definitely now with the Lord.

As he walked about thirty feet toward the burial location, I took up a spot directly across from where the priest would be standing, at the head of the casket. I was holding my Bible in my hand, but I also had to support Joan.

A week after Lee's funeral, I led Joan to the Lord too. She was baptized in the same church where Lee's service had been held. From then on, I took Joan to all of her doctor's appointments, blood work appointments and surgeries, and we spent quite a bit of time together.

But Joan, like Lee, was addicted to pain medication. She had been abused by a boyfriend of many years and suffered back pain and neck pain, had problems with her pancreas, high blood pressure, and she was also diabetic. On two separate occasions, I had to call an ambulance to come and get her, and she was taken to the hospital because her blood sugar had dipped too low.

Joan ended up in a small assisted-living facility where she was badly treated. I took her to the States Attorney's office, and we were in the process of filing charges against one of the women who worked in that facility. But three days later, Joan was found dead in her bed. It was another sad situation.

God had led me to these two sisters, who had been so terribly abused, and He had blessed them both, only to have them both die so tragically. At least He had made sure they were led to Him before their deaths.

I thank You, Lord, that I was able to bring joy to their lives. I thank You for choosing me to deliver the message of the cross to them. Thank You, for, as You taught me, I taught them. Today I know where they are, and I thank You for putting them in my life.

Another Catholic I led to the Lord was James. He, too, had been raised in the Catholic church and attended a Catholic school. This was not unusual.

Southern Maryland has always been primarily Roman Catholic. At the founding of this part of the state, a cross was raised at St. Clements Island, to claim the whole area for God and the church. Like Lee and Joan, James had never received Jesus as His Lord and Savior, so I had the privilege of leading him to salvation.

Then one day I had gone to the Charles County Library in La Plata to revisit old classic books about the early Four Square Gospel Church in Maryland. I was doing a study on Aimee Simple McPherson, and, because they were so old, the books I was gleaning from were not allowed to be taken out of the building. Sometimes I would spend hours there in the library in utter amazement, getting as much information as I could, to teach others from.

As I was leaving that day, I opened the car door to get in, when the Holy Spirit told me to go across the street to Civista Hospital. I got in the car and drove over to the hospital. Then the Holy Spirit said, "You are to volunteer."

I went into the volunteer office on the first floor and filled out the necessary paperwork. I had just recently completed an FBI background check, because of teaching special contract classes at high schools in

Prince Georges County. Locally I was volunteering at the detention center, so I had no problem with a background check. I had the needed paperwork in the dashboard compartment of my SUV.

They issued me several salmon-colored smocks and the logo appliques to iron on them. Then my picture was taken, and an official badge was issued. I actually worked several hours the next day doing data entry in one of the hospital's departments.

When I went home that day I waved at my next door neighbors, Jim and Sandy. "How are you doing, Jim?" I asked.

"Not so great," he answered.

As I walked toward him, I asked, "What's the problem?"

I couldn't help but notice how much weight Jim had lost, but he'd had several deaths in his family over that past year from cancer, so it didn't surprise me.

"They seem the think I have cancer," he told me now. "I'll be at Civista tomorrow to have tests run. Hopefully it will prove them wrong."

"Jim," I said, "I volunteer at the hospital. Do you mind if I come down and sit with Sandy tomorrow?"

While I was saying this, I was thinking, "Just look at You, God! This is why You had me go across the street from the library to volunteer."

"That would be great," Jim said "My appointment is at 9 a.m., so I'll see you then."

Jim and Sandy had been wonderful neighbors for more than twenty some years. Bill and I could always count on them to be there when we needed a helping hand. Now they needed me.

The next day at the hospital I sat with Sandy for a few minutes and talked and then I asked if she would mind if I went and checked on Jim.

"No," she said, "go right ahead."

I went back and found Jim, and we had time to talk. He, too, had been raised Catholic, and now I led him to the knowledge of salvation in Christ. Surely this was the reason God had told me to volunteer at the hospital.

Within a very few weeks, Jim was dead, and Sandy and her son were left devastated. I made a couple of platters full of assorted sandwiches and took them over to their house. They were race-car and race-boat enthusiasts, and were well known throughout the county.

The son, Little Jimmy (who was not little at all), always called me The Flying Nun, I guess because of my love for the Lord and the fact that I often mentioned His name in conversation. In reality, Little Jimmy was making fun of me, but I didn't take offense at it.

A few days after the funeral, I tried talking with Sandy about her salvation, but she was very angry. She was blaming God for Jim's death. I tried to explain that her happy marriage to the love of her life had been a gift from God. He had brought them together, but she could not be consoled.

One month later, Little Jimmy died of a heart attack there at home. Still, Sandy ignored me at every turn. Even when I would see her in the grocery store, she would turn her back, thinking maybe I wouldn't see her. I could not help but feel sorry for her. She was very lonely and very lost, and I knew she needed God in her life.

God loves His children so very much. Only He can fill the void, the emptiness that we all experience before we know Him. He is our Father, our friend, and the Lover of our soul.

Now I was led to back off. The seed had been planted, and it was God's work from here. I wanted to help my neighbor get through her pain, but it wasn't meant to be.

> *"Father, Isaiah said, 'I will trust and not be afraid.'* [9] *This is what I pray for Sandy: I pray that she will put all her trust in You, oh Lord, and not be afraid, for You are always there with her.*

I cannot be certain of my neighbor's salvation. What I do know is that she is now in an assisted-living facility suffering from dementia. I leave her in God's capable hands. That's all I can do.

I was *Maturing in Sonship through Suffering.*

---

9. This prayer is based on Isaiah 12:2.

✝ ✝ ✝

What is the Calling of the Believer?

We are not called upon

To imitate Christ.

We are called to learn how

To let the very life of Christ

Flow through us.

Only then can we truly be

Exhibiting Christ.

Become like Christ,

Have the mind of Christ,

Walk and exhibit divine attributes

That come from

The working of the Spirit

We are to exhibit Christ

To the world in which we live!

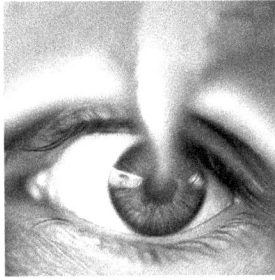

My Love Child

Thou shalt keep therefore His statutes and His commandments which I command thee this day, that it may go well with thee and with thy children after thee. Deuteronomy 4:40

I gave birth to a son and called him Jeffrey. The doctor had just delivered him and handed him off to a nurse to be cleaned, when I noticed that his foot seemed to be twisted. "What's wrong with my baby's foot?" I asked.

"He's okay," the doctor replied.

But a few hours later nurses brought Jeffrey to my room, and the doctor was with them. He explained that Jeffrey had a clubfoot and said they would begin trying to correct this deformity with casting. Jeffrey would leave the hospital with his left foot in a cast up to his knee.

Babies grow very fast, so the cast had to be checked every two weeks. The old casts were cut off with a circular saw (the noise of this alone was frightening for the child and his parents), and then a new cast was put on him. This was then done monthly, and the times were extended, depending on the Jeff's growth.

At the time, my husband was in the U.S. Coast Guard, stationed at Gwyn's Island, Virginia, so we used Langley Air Force Base Hospital in the Hampton Roads area. It was a great hospital with great doctors.

I held Jeff a lot, and there was a special bond I could feel with him. At first, I thought it was probably because my first son had died, I had lost three other children, and I was pouring out on Jeffrey the love I had lost with them. But this was something different. There was something special there that God was showing me. I called Jeffrey my child sent from Heaven and wrote a poem for him with that same title.

When Jeffrey was six months old I noticed a twitching or jerking motion in his body. I immediately drove him to the hospital, where he was admitted for observation.

By the third day, the doctor said he was going to release Jeff because they had found nothing wrong. I knew this was a mistake. When I was there or held him, I still noticed the twitching. After speaking with the nurses and the doctor, I asked if they could keep him one more night. They agreed for Jeff's crib to be kept at the nurse's station for a more complete observation. Until then, he had been in a room by himself, attended to only as required.

That afternoon, evening and night, Jeffrey was under constant observation, and twenty-seven *petit mal* seizures were noted in his chart. The next morning a medical flight was arranged for Jeffrey (and me), to be flown to Bethesda Naval Hospital in Maryland. There he was to undergo thirty days of neurological workup. The findings were that he had *petit mal* epileptic seizures, with some slowness in activity, to suggest mild retardation.

At the age of three, Jeff finally got out of the cast and began to walk. But, because of almost constant seizures, it was difficult for him to have any type of attention span. When I held him, without looking in his eyes, I could feel something moving inside of his head, as if the skin over the scalp would move. When I told the doctors this, they just looked at me in disbelief. But I knew what I knew.

Jeffrey's seizures would sometimes begin with him gazing into space, his eyes going from side to side without his head moving. In the books I read on epilepsy, this was called "twitching." I found that it was a common feature for the eyes of epileptics to be drawn toward light. When outside, it would be sunlight. Inside, it could be a lamp or an overhead light. To combat this, Jeff, at a very young age, began wearing sunglasses and a cap with a visor on it to prevent further damage to his system. I always had to explain this to those who worked with him, so they would allow him to wear his sunglasses in class.

During my early months of pregnancy for Jeff, I had been treated for panic attacks with librium, a tranquillizer. Years later, it was discovered that librium caused birth defects. From that point on, it was placed in a high risk category for pregnant women. But this knowledge came too late for Jeffery. The damage was already done.

Now, when he would stand and begin to take steps, if Jeff's eyes would begin twitching back and forth, I would know he was about to fall and could run and catch him. He had a special walker made for him and also a custom-made helmet to prevent him from hitting his head when he fell. This allowed him the freedom he needed to practice learning to walk without hurting himself.

When Jeffrey was just eighteen months old, his little sister was born. We named her Jodie, after her dad, whose name was Joe.

Joe named both of his children. Jeffrey was named Jeffrey Carson. When I asked Joe why he had chosen that name, he said it was after Jefferson Davis and Kit Carson. He was a Southerner, from the Shenandoah Valley of Virginia, a little town called Woodstock.

Jodie was such a beautiful baby, perfect in every way. She seemed to know that her brother needed all this special attention, and so she was not at all demanding.

Joe had grown up attending Sunday School in the Methodist Church in Toms Brook, Virginia. I wanted to have our wedding ceremony in a church where he would feel comfortable and where he would then accompany me to services on Sundays. So we got married in the Methodist church.

From the moment I had met the Lord, I dreamed of that perfect family attending church together. I wanted a family that prayed together, attended church together and went to all the functions together. I wanted the family I had heard Billy Graham talking about. I wanted that love that reached beyond understanding.

I had two more pregnancies after Jodie was born. Both were sons, and, with both, I was unable to carry them to full term. Jodie had been perfect at birth, as were my other girls. My problem seemed to be that I was unable to give birth to a normal male child. Right or wrong, I attributed this to being damaged by being tossed down the steps when I was carrying my first male child. I may never know for sure, and I don't really want to know. That pain is long gone.

This second marriage was also far from perfect. I did not have a husband who would go to church with me, and there were always other women in the picture, even from the beginning. It just took me many years to confront what had been going on all along. I had so wanted the marriage to be perfect, but it was anything but.

Then things got worse. Joe's mother, Carrie, moved in with us. During the riots in Washington, D.C., she had lost her job and was forced to move. Since she had nowhere else to go, she moved in with us. My initial thought was, "That's good. She can watch the children, and I'll be able to get a job." But I wasn't sure because I didn't really know her all that well. As it turned out, neither did her own son. Joe had been raised by his Aunt June and Uncle Harry.

Back in the 1950s, 60s and 70s, there was no family assistance help from the counties or states. There were no food stamps, no housing allowances, no welfare or other public assistance of any other kind for many. When husbands left their wives, most women were helpless. They had never been trained for the workplace. Months and years would go by before the courts would even force husband to support their children.

This was also the time when divorce became more liberal, and one could get divorced because of cruelty or physical abuse. So, during the 1970s, many women left their abusive situations, but often the children had to be raised by family members ... until some other arrangements could be made.

When Carrie moved in with us, I was happy for Joe. For the first time, he would have a mother in his life. But Carrie was not the mother, nor the grandmother we had hoped for. She had lived alone for many years. She had worked very hard during the days, and when she went home (which was over a pizza shop in Southeast D.C., her relaxation was watching television nonstop and drinking until she fell asleep. It didn't take long to realize that she would not be a suitable babysitter for the children.

Now, with no work to go to, Carrie sat in a chair in front of the television from sunup to midnight. She was amazing, drinking a quart of whiskey (Canadian Mist), every day and eating two boxes of Bugles as an accompaniment. The result was that she weighed in at over four hundred pounds.

Every night, Carrie fell asleep in font of the television, and Joe had to wake her up and tell her it was time to go to bed. This was all causing friction in the marriage, because now everything centered around her, rather than around our children.

Because I could not leave the children with their grandmother, Joe felt he had to take on an extra job, and the job he found was at the Chiefs Club on base. For all intents and purposes, it was a bar, and this only added to the strain on our marriage.

Not all of our troubles were Joe's fault. I had built up so many walls around myself that it was hard for him or anyone else to get close to me. Now Jodie and Jeff were my life.

For several reasons, it was very difficult for us to get any suitable childcare. Jeffrey was a handful, so I didn't dare leave him or Jodie with my mother-in-law. When he had been diagnosed in early childhood with moderate to severe retardation, those who made the diagnosis said that there was the distinct possibility that he would not live past the age of fourteen.

Eventually, with all of these strains, our marriage came to an end, and I moved in with my parents in Maryland again. Joe would call sometimes and check on the children. He told me his mother had moved and was living with a niece.

After about six to eight months of this, he asked me to come back. I agreed, but only if he would transfer out of the Norfolk/Portsmouth, Virginia area. There was too much painful history there.

He put in for a transfer to Galveston, Texas, and things were looking up. We found a special school there for Jeffery, and Jodie started first grade there. I joined a small Baptist church in Hitchcock, Texas, and began teaching Sunday school.

Then Joe started working weekends at the club on base, and old habits rose up again. We separated again, and I began working as well. I rented a small restaurant/bar in Alta Loma, Texas, and was able to keep the children with me. But, after just six months, I realized that I could not work and take care of them at the same time, so I headed back home to Maryland. Thank God for loving parents!

There was so much to love about them. Dinner was on the table at the same time every night when Dad came home from work. We always went somewhere on the weekends, to the zoo or on picnics. It was a big disappointment to me not to have had what I perceived as the perfect family, but when you get married at fifteen, and you are still a child yourself, and when you have three children before you are nineteen, that's a lot to expect.

Today, as I look back through very different eyes, I am so grateful for my children. Jeffrey is a man now, living in a community with other people with disabilities, and he is very happy. He is able to come home often, since he lives only fifteen minutes away.

Jodie, who works as a loan officer in a bank, is the mother of four adult children—John, Joe, Jessica and Tommy—and one grandchild, Danielle Elizabeth. Jodie is in a happy relationship with Mike.

Jeneene, my oldest daughter, is a registered nurse and has an apartment near me.

Catherine, my next to the oldest, is happily married and works for the government, has dogs and horses and a wonderful husband, also named Mike.

My third daughter, Terry (Theresa Christine) died either of a drug overdose or because of taking bad drugs. No one was ever sure which. She was found on the bathroom floor of a pool hall at 4 a.m. on a Monday morning. Two young girls were injecting each other with drugs. One of them lived, and the other one died.

I was sitting in a classroom at our local community college, where I was taking classes in accounting, when a police officer walked through the door, coming to tell me of my daughter's death.

Two of my first four children were now gone. I worried for years over their salvation and prayed that God would allow me to hold them when I got to Heaven. I had cried for so many years for the souls of my children and know that my son Ross went into the arms of Jesus the moment he passed over.

With Terry, I had read many of her writings and poems and know that she believed in Jesus, but in her teenage years she also dabbled in the occult. I pray that there was a moment when she accepted Christ.

It is amazing how we build up walls of protection around ourselves in life, not wanting anyone else to hurt us or our children, trying to make the right decisions for all concerned, but often reacting badly in frantic situations, not weighting out the possible outcomes. But now, the hatred, the blame game and unforgiveness that I had felt toward my first and second husbands for so many years was gone. And the walls I had built to protect myself had been torn down.

It is amazing how smothering hatred can be and what it did to me. I thank God for forgiveness. Not only that He forgives us, but that He has shown me how to forgive others and how to forgive myself.

It is not always easy to forgive, but when we don't do it, we hurt ourselves and our children more than anyone else. God wants to set us free from all old grievances and harbored resentments. He will heal our broken hearts, if we just let Him. He will create in us a new heart:

Jesus set the example for us. He prayed:

Father, forgive them for they know not what they do!   Luke 23:24

And that's what you and I must do as well.

Father, You told the apostle Paul that Your grace was all he needed and that Your power is made perfect in weakness. [10]
Father, I know that Your grace is sufficient for me and for my children. I say, "For as for me and my house, we will serve the Lord," forever.

I was *Maturing in Sonship through Suffering.*

---

10. This prayer is based on God's promise in 2 Corinthians 12:9.

According to His Word, God will not withhold anything good from us, providing we meet three conditions laid out for us. The promise is simple, complete and easy to understand:

1. Fear the Lord
2. Seek the Lord
3. Walk Uprightly

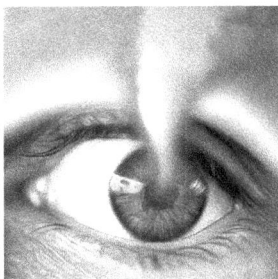

~ Nineteen ~

Releasing Your Yesterdays

Ye shall receive power, after that the Holy Ghost is come upon you; and ye shall be witnesses unto Me.   Acts 1:8

Only when you have released your yesterdays will you receive the promises of tomorrow. You will know without a doubt when the presence of the Holy Spirit has come upon your life. You will also know when He has empowered you—spiritually, mentally and physically. You have been equipped with the promise and the power of the anointing of the Holy Spirit for a purpose, with signs following. You may not see the Spirit coming, but you certainly know when He has been there.

After I had been filled with the Holy Spirit with the evidence of speaking in tongues, it was apparent to me immediately that He had also empowered me, to the point that I truly thought I would die or explode from within. It was almost similar to an anxiety attack, where something is happening to you, yet you have no control over the situation. There was so much of the anointing that I asked God to take some back of it, knowing I was not able to handle it all. It was overwhelming, unexplainable and wonderful, yet somehow frightening at the same time. That is where complete surrender comes into play. I can say that it was a life-changing moment, and my life has never been the same since.

It takes time to learn to flow in the new gifts and the signs that will follow. The Bible says our witness to Christ can be confirmed *"with signs following"* (Mark 16:20). The presence of God is His glory. Often tears will seep from your eyes or roll down your cheeks as you are overcome with this glorious presence.

The Shekinah glory is heavy, and often it becomes hard for you to stand or even move in His presence. I close my eyes and whisper His glorious name—Jesus, Jesus, Jesus!

The anointing is the power, the power to serve God. I knew I had been transformed forever. And today I still believe that, as He continues to use me and move me.

He has given this gift to you and wants you at His call. Pray when He says pray, go where He tells you to go, and do what He tells you to do. You may question whether it is truly Him, but never refuse, or He may never use you again. That is the price you must pay to be one of His chosen ones.

Listen for His voice and do whatever is asked. We must be willing to pay the price of obedience.

Oh, Lord, please never take your Holy Spirit from me! I surrender my life to You, forever.

Living in this state of obedience is what God asks of each of us. It is also where I long to be. The anointing is the Holy Spirit, and I am longing to spend hours alone with Him, to draw closer to Him with each day, telling Him how much I love Him. He is glorious. This is my desire, to be wrapped up in Him and His love.

When the Holy Spirit is a reality in your life, He provides an avenue through which the anointing, the power, can flow. We are the vessels, but it is what is in the vessel, what is within, the power, that makes all the difference.

And what is within? It's the Holy Spirit. It's not you; it's Him. Remain little in your own eyes. Lose sight of yourself, and gain sight of God.

I have often wondered what others saw in me or on me when I was filled with the Holy Ghost. They were drawn by something. That African-American woman at Giant Food store that I spoke of in another chapter was drawn to me, a total strange, a white woman. What drew her?

When I was still attending the Baptist Church in southern Maryland, one of the teens seemed to be drawn to me. She wanted to talk about her parents, for they were having problems with their marriage. This young girl didn't really know me, yet the Spirit drew her to me. We began communicating though e-mail, and I began praying for her family. At a certain point, God told me to confide in the pastor about their needs. I did this. To my knowledge, no one else in the church knew what was happening, but the marriage was saved.

Weeks later, a middle-aged married man came to me, telling me his wife was seeing another man, someone she worked with. He had been told by the Holy Spirit to check her cellphone and that was how he found out about the affair. We began praying and continued to communicate and pray together about it for the next few weeks. Again, God told me to go to the pastor, and I did. That marriage was saved too, and the family remained intact.

Month's later, one of the women attending my ladies' Sunday morning Bible study class asked if I would pray for her grandson who had been diagnosed with leukemia. Our class began praying, and we prayed for months for this young seven-year-old.

I began teaching on the indwelling of the Holy Spirit, and this woman was Spirit filled. She then laid hands on her grandson, and he was healed. Praise God! The Holy Spirit draws people to you, and works through you, to intervene on behalf of the Father.

Our greatest desire should not be for spiritual gifts, but for the presence and the power of God. Gifts may not change your life, but His presence and power surely will.

I will put My Spirit within you and cause you to walk in My statutes, and you will keep My judgements and do them. Ezekiel 36:27

But you shall receive power when the Holy Spirit has come upon you; and you shall be witnesses to Me in Jerusalem, and in all Judea and Samaria, and to the end of the earth. Acts 1:8, NKJV

Release your yesterdays and get lost in your tomorrows in God! As for me, I was *Maturing in Sonship through Suffering.*

Fear the Lord

Psalm 34:9, KJV

O fear the LORD,
ye his saints:
for there is no want
to them that fear him.

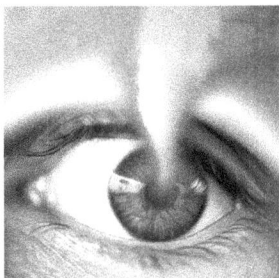

The Father Weeps

Jesus wept.   John 11:35

It was a beautiful spring day, as I began driving toward Washington, D.C. The sky was about three different shades of pastel blue, with white fluffy clouds moving slowly over it all. I was beginning a new teaching assignment in the inner city that morning, teaching workforce development to high school dropouts, at-risk youth and recovering adults.

As I turned off of Atlantic Street SE onto 8th Street, I began looking for an elementary school. The building where I would be teaching would be in the rear fenced-in area, behind the school.

221

Spotting the school, I pulled into the parking lot and began observing the area, wanting to see which door I should enter. Having grown up in the inner city, I was street wise and cautious.

I had pulled into the parking lot facing the basketball/playground area. What immediately caught my eye was a huge mural that spanned the width of the basketball court. It had been painted there up high for all in the area to see. It was intended as a message to a downtrodden neighborhood, an encouragement to all those who would play sports there, and it was to lift up the children who attended the school through the years.

Arthur Ashe was in the picture, showing his tennis backhand.[11] There were also basketball greats, track stars, boxers such as Sugar Ray[12] and Joe Lewis,[13] and other well known athletes. But,

11. Arthur Robert Ashe, Jr. (July 10, 1943 – February 6, 1993) was an American World No. 1 professional tennis player. He won three Grand Slam titles, ranking him among the best tennis players from the United States.
12. Ray Charles "Sugar Ray" Leonard (born May 17, 1956) is an American former professional boxer, motivational speaker, and occasional actor.
13. Joseph Louis Barrow, best known as Joe Louis, was an American professional boxer. He held the world heavyweight championship from 1937 to 1949, and is considered to be one of the greatest heavyweights of all time.

like many inner-city areas, graffiti had been add-ed to the well-planned and executed project. Filthy three- and four-letter words had also been spay painted predominantly.

Tears began to well up in my eyes, as I thought of the little children who spent recess trying to sound out those one-syllable words, and I began writing down the different color paints I would need to cover them over. This had really struck me hard, and I was not certain why.

A car pulled into the lot and parked about two car spaces away from me. The windows were down, and filthy rap music was blaring so that you could almost see the car vibrating from the loudness of the music. The young teenage-looking mother be-hind the wheel of the car was moving with the mu-sic's beat. The saddest part was seeing two small children seated in their car seats in the back. As young as they were, they were mouthing the filthy words of the rap song. They were just four- or five-year-olds, and yet they knew every word to that song. Tears were flowing as my heart was breaking for the children.

What was wrong with me? I could not believe the reaction I was having to the mural and the rap music. My head turned to the right, just outside the gate entrance to the parking area. Three young teenagers were there. Two were loosening the lug nuts on a car, so they could steal the tires, while the third teen was removing the car's tags.

"Lord, what are You trying to tell me?" I prayed. "What is this all about? I know this is You. It has to be. All of this has transpired in ten minutes, and it isn't even 8:45 yet. Why are You showing me all of this, Lord?"

He replied in a very soft, yet sad voice, "These are the things that I look upon every day, all over the world." At that moment, I realized that God weeps for His children.

I was so filled with the Holy Spirit as I entered the class that day. I was shaking, but I was able to compose myself in front of the class.

After greeting the class, I introduced myself and these words came out of my mouth. "Get your life straight with God, for time is short." It was the Holy Spirit speaking through me. At that moment, I knew that it was a direct message from God, that my life had taken on a new direction, and that I would be used of God in new and mighty way.

Our God weeps for His children, and when we love Him and want to do His will on earth, we, too, will weep for those who suffer. For my part, I love Him so very much and would never want to hurt Him in any way.

It was all part of the process, and I was *Maturing in Sonship through Suffering*

Proverb 8:13, KJV

*The fear of the L*ORD *is to hate evil: pride, and arrogance, and the evil way, and the froward (perverse, deceitful) mouth do I hate.*

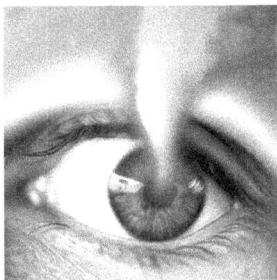

Rough Beginnings

Beware of false prophets, who come to you in sheep's clothing, but inwardly they are ravening wolves. Matthew 7:15

It is amazing how God puts people in our lives for a season and for a reason. Often they are used to strengthen our foundation in different areas. Their strong point may be our weak point, so we learn from each other. Often people will fail the test and begin dragging you down. When it happens, the Holy Spirit will remove them from your life immediately.

Sometimes life seems to be composed of back-stabbers, backbiters, and people wrapped up in self, and they all call themselves Christians, yet they use other people to advance themselves in different areas. Believe me, they will only be in your life for a short period. The Bible shows us that not everyone can get along with others. Some will join us on our ministry travels, and others will be left behind. We learn from our own mistakes, as well as the mistakes of others.

After the Lord had called me to teach and evangelize, He then called me to preach. I began teaching at woman's conferences in Maryland, Virginia and Washington, D.C. As noted earlier, my ministry was called Restoring the Broken Vessel and was aimed at helping abused women to free themselves of the unforgiveness in their lives through the Word of God. Even Jesus needed to forgive those who had taken part in His crucifixion. And He did forgive them.

While attending an Assembly of God church in Maryland, I met Revs. James and Fern Allen, who were both ordained under the Gospel Crusade Ministerial Fellowship in Stevens, Pennsylvania. After applying for membership in this organization, and passing and meeting all the requirements for their ministry, I was accepted into fellowship. My district office was located in Fredericksburg, Virginia, and was under Revs. Richard and Christine Dunk.

While preaching at a women's conference in Maryland, the Lord placed me with some very immature Christians who were having their first conference. Through this experience, the Lord showed me all the things not to do when setting up a conference and the importance of having planning meetings prior to the actual event.

We can never assume everyone is on the same page, and there are policies and procedures that must be discussed and followed. There is also a chain of command and an order that must be followed. When we wrong someone, an apology must follow. We are brothers and sisters in Christ, and this Christian life is not a competition.

In this case, I was only an observer, but because rules were not set down and discussed prior, I could see feathers being ruffled. Feelings were hurt, and because of it, some then went for years without speaking to each other. Some have even gone out of their way to try to ruin the ministry of others.

Fortunately the Lord placed a young energetic, on-fire Christian in my path. It was her first large conference. She was not told of the rules before hand, and she began ministering as soon as she arrived. She was approached by leadership and asked not to do that.

But the conference had not even started, and this woman just wanted to do the work of the Master. She was so filled with the power of God that people were lying about everywhere, and, again, the conference had not yet begun.

The members of the conference management team were on fire as well, but their fire was from anger. They were mad at the young on-fire evangelist and stopped talking to her, so she was left hanging.

When the programs were handed out, I found I was on the agenda as the third speaker on the first day. We did not realize it at the time, but God was orchestrating this whole conference in our favor.

I invited Rev. Kathleen Mae Walker and another fellow speaker, Pastor John, to my room for prayer and communion. Kathleen said she would first have to check into her room, and then she would join me. Within fifteen minutes she was back. It seemed that she and I would be sharing a room. This was great.

The three of us talked over the situation, and prayed for the others as well. We talked for what seemed like hours. Kathleen and John said how much they had enjoyed my presentation earlier in the day. "But," Kathleen said, "your content today is what I was going to talk on tomorrow, almost word for word. What should I do?"

I closed my eyes and prayed for a brief moment, waiting for the Holy Spirit to come through, and He did. "Kathleen, the Lord is telling me your teaching should be on love, Christian Love." Without any notes she gave the most sensitive and dramatic teaching on the subject of love I had ever heard. I personally don't know how she did it, but her teaching the next morning knocked it out of the ballpark. Unfortunately the minister that organized the conference have not spoken to Kathleen since then.

Rev. Kathleen is on fire for the Lord in Mbale Uganda, where she has married a native who was part of her ministry, and together they have also started a large orphanage called the House of Grace. At this writing, they have fourteen children.

They have purchased land, where they will build to enlarge the House of Grace and have their school of evangelism housed there as well They also have many other churches out in the bush area, and are in demand to speak throughout Uganda and many European countries under their name: "Fresh Revival Fire Ministries" (www.frfministries.org). You might want to check Kathleen out on Facebook\ Kathleen Mae Masuba.

I was learning a lot of hard and I was *Maturing in Sonship through Suffering.*

Seek the Lord:

**With all your heart
(Deuteronomy 4:29)**

**Continually
(1 Chronicles 16:11)**

**By humbling yourself
(2 Chronicles 7:14)**

By prayer

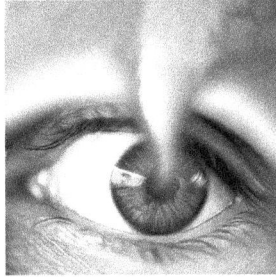

Favor in My Father's Eyes

But the Lord was with Joseph and showed him mercy, and gave him favor.   Genesis 39:21

I was excited, as I headed down the highway from Waldorf to Virginia Beach. It was a beautiful day, and the weekend was forecast to be the same. I would be staying at the Heritage Inn, which is well known to the Christian community.

Six tapes were set-up in my CD player, so I could listen to the teaching on the "Anointing" by Benny Hinn during my drive. Pastor Benny carries such a strong anointing that the moment I get near his venue or even to places associated with him or his ministry, I can feel the glorious presence of the Lord.

I checked in at the Heritage at 1 p.m., went to my room and unpacked my suitcase. My hair needed to be washed and blow-dried, so I went into the ladies' boutique there in the hotel and asked for directions to a hair stylist close by.

After returning to my room, I looked through the hotel directory for churches to be sure I had the correct address for Rock Church. While looking through the directory, I noticed that Rock Church had a Thursday night service at 7 p.m. "That can't be right," I thought. "Churches have mid-week services on Wednesday nights."

I decided to grab an early dinner and go to the service at Rock Church. The conference would not start until the next morning.

Surprisingly, there were not many cars in the parking lot at the church. I watched to see which of the many doors people were entering and followed them. Everyone was seated in the fifth or sixth row back on the left hand side of the platform. So I walked down the aisle toward them, sat down close by and joined in the conversation. "What time does the service start tonight?" I asked one of the ladies.

"Oh, there's no service tonight," she said, "we're here to practice for choir. Our service was Wednesday night, last night. Why don't you join in and sing with us tonight and then tomorrow?" she suggested.

"I would love to," I replied, "but I can't. Several nodules were removed from my vocal cords a few days ago, and that's why I'm here, to have Pastor Benny pray over me."

"Then let me bless you," she said. "I am a member of this church, and I have tickets that will allow you to sit up front. You can also come in an hour before the rest of the crowd. You will enter in the glass door on the left side of the building."

Tears began welling up in my eyes, as I realized that God had arranged all of this. The directory in the hotel room had been changed so that I would come to the church Thursday evening. He had led me to this wonderful woman who had given me her tickets to the Benny Hinn crusade. You cannot believe how excited I was when she handed me those tickets.

The next morning I arrived early, knowing the crowd would be huge, and not being sure how many members would be at that glass door ahead of me. I made my way through thousands of people to the opposite side of the building. Too late I realized that I could have parked on this side. When I got to the glass door, I was amazed. There was no one there but me. Praise God, praise God, praise God! I stood there, ticket in hand, smiling inside and saying, "Thank You, Lord! Thank You, Lord!"

I stood there by myself for at least twenty minutes, continually thanking the Lord, until I began wondering if I might be at the wrong door. Thousands of people were lined up on the other side of the building, and there, where I was, there was no one but me.

Then, suddenly, a car pulled up and dropped off a very petite lady. She stood with me, and we had wonderful conversation. We were both feeding off each other's anointing. It was great. Within a few minutes, twenty or thirty other people had arrived at the glass door.

Someone from the church staff came to the door and invited the woman I was standing with into the church. As she entered, she said, "I will save you a seat, Sheila. Look for me. I'll wave."

Another fifteen minutes passed, and the door was opened. As I entered, I looked around for my newfound friend. There she was, down front, and she was waving continuously. I motioned that I had seen her.

We began our conversations again. She was very excited to hear of the many spiritual revelations I had experienced and wanted to hear more. During our conversation, she told me she was the mother of one of the assistant pastors at Rock Church. About that time, her son came to make sure his mother was settled in okay. She introduced me to him, and we exchanged pleasantries. The mother and I exchanged addresses and phone numbers, and time flew by.

Benny Hinn Partners were now coming in, and the choir was on stage in cobalt blue attire, as they began to practice a few of their songs. It seemed only minutes before the massive church was filled. Others would be going to the overflow buildings. But here I was. I had found favor in my Father's eyes! How mighty is my God! He is my God, my God, my God.

Now people were standing as they worshiped, hands in the air in total surrender. The music was beautiful, the crowd was electric, and the presence of God was glorious. As the air conditioner was

239

turned up, and the choir began to sing *Alleluia* (if you have ever been to a Benny Hinn conference, at that moment you knew he was on stage). Eyes began to search for him in his pure white suit, as he began to sing *Alleluia* with the choir. It was a pure worship, and you could feel how much the Lord loves that song. Tears began to seep from my eyes. Some were unable to stand under the anointing. It was wonderful.

The healing lines began to form, and I walked up toward the steps. They asked in what area I needed prayer, and I explained that I'd had surgery on my vocal cords and needed prayer for complete healing. The surgeons report was not back yet, so I was just asking for complete healing.

Benny touched me so very gently in the throat area and said, "Lord, give her complete healing. Lord give her more of You." About that time, I hit the floor and must have remained there ten to twenty minutes, and then Pastor Benny had his staff pick me up.

My feet were a little unsteady. "What are you feeling?" he asked.

I smiled and said, "It's wonderful, it's just wonderful."

Once again he touched my throat and said, "Bye, bye!"

The test results of the biopsy came back negative, and that was great.

Thank You, Lord. You are the God that heals those who cry out!

I was *Maturing in Sonship through Suffering.*

Seek the Lord:

_____

By turning from sin

By preparing the heart
(2 Chronicles 19:3)

Diligently seek Him
(Hebrews 11:6).

Hosea 10:12
*For it is time to
seek the L*ORD *until
He come and rain
righteousness upon
you* [the seeker].

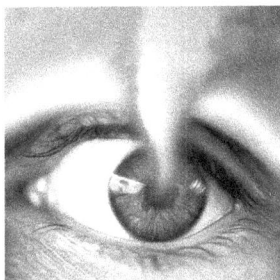

~ TWENTY-THREE ~

Private Time with God

For in the time of trouble He shall hide me in His
pavilion; in the secret places of His tabernacle shall
He hide me; He shall set me upon a rock.

Psalm 27:5

As I traveled over the Chesapeake Bay Bridge, driving toward the Eastern Shore of Maryland, I was not certain where I was going to stop. My intention had been to get out of the house for a few days. I needed time away from a busy phone and people dropping by. I needed a peaceful change of scenery and time alone with the Lord. When our lives get busy with things, it often becomes very difficult to have time alone with the Lord

I felt that I was doing the work of the Lord, reaching out to those in need in the inner-city. But it's one thing to do the work of the Lord and another to have a true relationship with Him. We must be hearing His voice, listening intently with a surrendered heart.

Often, when we become ministers, doing the work of the Lord, starting our own church and doing what we feel we have been called to do, that relationship suffers because we become too involved in the day-to-day details. Yes, we pray, but do we truly seek God's face? Do we truly humble ourselves, giving Him our all, our private time, free of the junk of the world. Or, when praying, do we stop to answer the phone and do other things the enemy uses to distract us?

I needed that private time and a place where I could seek God's face and receive what He had for me at that moment. I needed a breakthrough where I knew He was working something out in my life. I needed Him to empty me of self and then fill me once more. I wasn't sure exactly what I needed, but I knew I needed to spend private time with God.

There was a second reason for my outing that day. Bill had recently passed away, and I needed to mourn his passing. I had been so busy caring for him day and night, and now he was gone, and I'd had no time to grieve. This was to be my time.

Looking back now, I cannot remember exactly where I stopped. I do remember that it was raining, and I had a side view of the Atlantic Ocean. I got a room for the night.

I threw a blanket on the floor and lay prostrate on it, crying out to God, seeking direction. Loneliness had somehow taken over my spirit. I was totally alone for the first time in twenty-five years. Even my twelve-year-old Jack Russell had recently died. I knew the Holy Spirit was with me, but I needed someone to talk with.

I cannot say just how long I lay on the floor of the hotel room. I do remember that I fell asleep in my tears.

When I awoke the Lord led me to Ezekiel 26 and 27 and I heard the words within me, "You are to step out and speak out to edify the Church, pulling down strongholds. Utilize the power you have been given. Prophesy over hopeless situations. You have the authority to do the work of the Lord.

"Prophesy over hopeless situations by calling things that are not as though they were. Those who

245

are hungry shall be filled. Believe in what you have been promised. What I have, I have given you. Now, you are to step out and use My name, for in My name the power remains and will remain forever!"

I had a choice. I could stand by and watch the church die, or I could obey God and call down things that are not, as though they were. His promise is that when any two agree, what they declare shall be done. I was to prophesy over hopeless situation, over the dead, dry bones of the church.

I had to heed His call, remain watchful and diligent, and fully dedicate my love, faithfulness and trust to the Father. And that's what I have done ever since.

The psalmist declared:

O God, You are my God;
Early will I seek You;
My soul thirsts for You;
My flesh longs for You
In a dry and thirsty land
Where there is no water.
So I have looked for You in the sanctuary,
To see Your power and Your glory

Psalm 63:1-2, NKJV

246

God is looking for those who will come to the place of absolute surrender. He really starts to use men and women when they become totally consumed by Him.

I am consumed by You, my Lord. My thirst seems to never be quenched, my hunger for more of You is never filled. I long for more of You every waking hour. As I fall asleep each night, I seek Your face. I seek You constantly in the Word and in my prayer closet, praying in the Spirit.

In every way I was *Maturing in Sonship through Suffering.*

We Must Walk Uprightly

Psalm 84:11
No good thing will He withhold from them that walk uprightly.

Walk in the way of God's judgments (Isaiah 26:8).

Wait for the Lord to lead.

Desire the name of God.

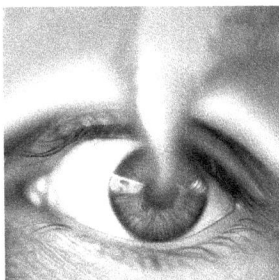

Continually Thanking God

Keep me as the apple of Your eye;
Hide me under the shadow of Your wings,
From the wicked who oppress me,
From my deadly enemies who surround me.

Psalm 17:8-9

Recently the Lord answered my frantic call for a new pet companion and gave me an eight-week-old cock-a-poo. I named him Boo. I decided to take him out one day to teach him to walk on a leash. After we had walked out to the street to retrieve our trash can, we turned to walk back down the driveway, and suddenly there stood a pit bull staring at my pup like he was lunch.

I avoided making eye contact with the pit, but I immediately screamed out for his caregiver, a neighbor. Bob came running from his backyard, where he had been walking two other dogs. But before he could get to us, the full-grown pit bull opened his mouth wide and locked it over the entire head of my pup.

"My God! My God, help me!" I screamed.

The pit released the grip he had on the puppy, and I opened the lid of the trash can, yanked my beautiful pup up by the leash, and threw him inside and closed the lid. I hadn't even thought about it. It was God!

As I began to wheel the trash can away, the pit lunged toward my hands. I was able to move my hands away in time, and his teeth clamped down on the huge heavy plastic receptacle handle. I turned the can around and began backing down the driveway, pulling the trash can with me. By this time, Bob had arrived, and he lunged for the pit.

I began shouting for my oldest daughter Jeneene, who lives in a small house behind me. She opened the door and pulled in the huge trash can, not realizing why.

"Call 911," I cried out, as tears of relief began to flow down my cheeks. "Bob, next door, is being attacked by his dog. Tell them to send an ambulance. He's covered with blood. And tell them it's a pit bull."

Bob had somehow managed to get the dog in the garage, just as the ambulance pulled in the driveway, followed by Animal Rescue teams. He was taken to a local hospital but was then transported to Johns Hopkins in Baltimore for surgery. The dog had caused a great deal of damage to his right eye and his scalp up through his hairline. He also had to have stitches in his arm and hands.

Boo had two puncture wounds to his head, one behind the ear and another on the soft spot of the head, and there was some swelling. But the Lord had saved the dog's life, and I had walked away without a scratch.

I praise You, Lord! I give You all the glory!

My neighbors were there with cash money to pay for all the vet bill's and check on Boo during the duration of his treatment.

A few weeks later the same pit bull attacked Bob once again. This time he went for his face, messing up his chin and his teeth and affecting his speech. I can also see that Bob's spirit has been broken though all of this. I will continue to hold Bob up in prayer, and continually thank God for saving our lives.

Lord I continue to seek Your presence and to constantly surrender myself to You. When I call, You are there. You said in Your Word. "I will never leave you nor forsake you." If You said it, I believe it! We must learn to read Your promises daily and to stand on them. We must put our faith in You. We must be controlled by the Spirit, not by circumstances or by unbelief.
I love You, Lord, today, tomorrow and forever! Thank You for loving me.

My words for all those reading this would be: Go Deeper! Draw closer to the Lord. Talk to Him, and He will answer. God is so very real. He is alive. He is a person, and He longs to live inside each of us.

He is at the door even now. Invite Him in. His promises are for you as well as me. He only asks that you believe!

God was true to His Word. He hid me (and Boo) under the shadow of His wings. I was *Maturing in Sonship through Suffering.*

We Must Walk Uprightly

Remembering the Lord

Desiring the Lord with your whole soul (Isaiah 26:9)

Seeking God early with your spirit

Learning righteousness through chastening (Isaiah 26:9 and Hebrews 12:5-13)

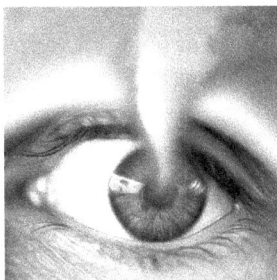

~ TWENTY-FIVE ~

In Conclusion

Then he brought me back to the door of the temple; and there was water, flowing from under the threshold of the temple toward the east, for the front of the temple faced east; the water was flowing from under the right side of the temple, south of the altar.   Ezekiel 47:1

We are currently watching the rivers of living water breaking out in many directions around the world. Those of us who walk with the Lord can feel the heaviness of something that is about to come. We walk not in fear, for He is with us.

The divine Spirit has been working at an increased pace that seems to be intensifying almost daily. Many of us are reading, studying, and digging new wells in the Word as never before.

Just prior to September 11,ʹ there was an awakening. Since then, we see that churches have changed. Home churches have increased, prayer groups, phone-line prayer, the prophetic and prophetic round-tables have also increased. We are longing for more of Him and experiencing an unquenchable thirst, a hunger that never seems to leave us.

Although many of the organized religions seem to be falling away because of man's doctrine, many others are seeking truth and longing to live for God. We have been given power, yet we feel powerless and many lack even the assurance of salvation. We have been seeing a falling away from the things of God, but now the time has come for a falling away of the things of this world within us, a total surrender, an emptying of self. Our God is seeking an empty and yielded vessel He can work through.

In the days to come, services will be so extraordinary that people will lose all consciousness of time and place, the minister will forget his prepared sermon and rely on the Holy Spirit, and we will all be used in a remarkable manner. We must prepare for the tidal wave that will burst over us and the land, for it will be a time for congregations to grow exponentially, until their facilities are unable to accommodate any more worshipers.

As I described early on, I was purged when the light entered my eyes. The filth and the sludge was thrown from my body, out through both eyes, making a place inside of me for the Spirit to dwell. Then the Spirit settled in on my left side, just below my last bottom rib. He is with me always. He promised:

If My people who are called by My name will humble themselves, and pray and seek My face, and turn from their wicked ways, then I will hear from heaven, and will forgive their sin and heal their land.   2 Chronicles 7:14

Lord, today we call on You in repentance and faith, seeking Your face continuously, with love and longing, praying that You will let this be a chosen and sanctified house, and that Your eyes will ever search our hearts as we draw closer to You, loving You more and more each day. And we will love You forever.
Amen!

Prayers to the Father

Good morning, Father, I begin this day that You have blessed me with, in prayer, to give You praise and glory and honor, to give You all the love I have to give. Blanket me with Your love this day, I pray. Watch over me and my family, my children, and grandchildren and great-grandchildren, with total protection from obstacles and the evil people of this world. Protect us with Your wall of protection, as we travel throughout the day. Put others in our path whom You would have us witness to.

I am only the vessel, Oh Lord, and I empty myself out, making room for Your Holy Spirit, for I can do nothing without You.

The Holy Spirit is the treasure within the vessel. I have filled myself with Your words, Lord, that Your Spirit may bring it to my remembrance. Let Your light emit from me and draw others closer to You.

And through my vessel, when my hand reaches out to touch others, let that touch be Your touch.

When I reach out with love, let it be Your love. And when the anointing, the river, flows out of me, continually fill me back up. For it is not the vessel, but what is within the vessel and what comes out that counts. When we truly follow the Spirit of God, we are Sons of God, so You are my Life. You are my Love. You are all I desire.

In Jesus' name, that name above all names.

§

Holy Father, as I go throughout the day traveling to work or going about daily chores in traffic, I ask for Your total protection. Also protect me from the evil one, for the mind is not saved from Satan. Let me keep it focused on the Word of God. Help me to do spiritual exercises to form my mind — remembering the books of the Bible, the disciples, the twelve tribes of Israel, and special verses. This will all keep me focused on You, Lord.

Protect my eyes from seeing things they should not see, and close my ears to the ugly words and sayings of this world. As I turn on worship music in my car, know that it is for

You, my Lord. As I sing to You and speak to You in my special language, let the anointing fill the car, and prepare me for where I am going. Also, Father, prepare the hearts of the people I will be coming in contact with throughout this day.

I love You and worship You, I hunger for more of You, and I thirst for You. This is a hunger and thirst that seems to grow and can never be fully quenched. The more of You I get, the more of You I need and want.

Keep the light burning within the Church of today I pray. Please, Lord God, never take Your Spirit from me, for You are all I desire, and to please You is my goal, forever and always. Amen!

§

Good Morning, Father. I come to You in the name of Jesus. I come to You today to praise You, worship You and thank You for all You do, have done and will continue to do.

I thank You, Lord, for salvation. I thank You for lifting me from the miry clay, the sludge, mud and filth of the world. Thank You, Lord, for forgiveness; not only for forgiving me, but also for teaching me to forgive others. Thank You, Lord, for eternal salvation, for the joy of knowing we will spend eternity with You.

All tears and fears will be gone. All hurt and pain will be gone. We will be enveloped in a sea of Your love, goodness, kindness and peace. We will be free of sin, man-made medications and all the things that go with illness.

Thank You, God, in the name above every name. His name is Jesus!

About the Author

Born Sheila May Goldberg in Washington, D.C., the author was raised in a home that had no Bible. Her Father, Leo Goldberg, was born in Kansas, where his Jewish father had been murdered because of his heritage. Most of her dad's family was slaughtered in Germany during Hitler's massacres. Many of them lived in Goldberg, Germany, located in the northeastern part of the country, near the lake of the same name.

Sheila's mother, Ida Catherine Mattingly, was born in Avenue, Maryland (in the southern part of the state). She, like most resident families, was from England. Avenue was the location of the first Catholic Church formed in Maryland, and Ida and her nine siblings were raised strict Catholic.

Ida attended Holy Angels School and Church. Still, there was never a Bible in their home, only a Catholic Missal or book of prayers. Even these prayers were never shared with the family, but Sheila remembers her mother reading from the Missal daily. Ida Goldberg was a kind, gentle woman who loved the Lord, and her love was visible, but in those days she never shared her faith.

Sheila's calling is to share the Word of salvation to everyone she comes in contact with. Because of her many spiritual revelations, she knows without question that God is real. Whatever Satan means for evil, God uses for good.

She walks with God, talks with God and has an ongoing loving relationship with Him. He is the Light that shines on the path she follows.

Prior to their deaths, Sheila led both her mother and father to the Lord and purchased the first Bible for their home.

God has called Sheila as a watchman on the wall for the Church, sending her to churches He has selected. She observes, sometimes giving a word to the pastor. At other times, her anointing is to touch the congregation as a whole. She is excited and with a willing heart, to see what God has in store for her and where and what her next assignment will be.

Sheila is an ordained minister with Cross Country World Missions of Rocky Mount, North Carolina, and Gospel Crusades Fellowship, with headquarters in Stevens, Pennsylvania. She is also a Stevens Minister and Leader.

She is founder and Minister of Restoring the Broken Vessel Ministries, serving the District of Colombia, Maryland and Virginia, and ministers at women's conferences around the country. She teaches independently for Workforce Development, furnishing a stepping stone for at-risk youth and re-entry of the incarcerated back into the work place.

My Favorite Place
of Worship

My favorite place of worship is Calvary Pentecostal Campground in Ashland, Virginia, known by most simply as "the campground," where lodging and food are a gift from God. If you would like to attend the many wonderful activities at the camp, you may contact them directly:

www.calvarycampground.org

804.798.7756

Author Contact Page

Rev. Sheila Kay, Evangelist, Teacher and Visionary
Restoring the Broken Vessel Ministries
is available for conferences, seminars, retreats,
and women's groups

As a Certified Dietary Manager and Food Service
Consultant, she certifies church food service workers
nationally as Certified Professional Food Managers
(Food Sanitation and HACCP)

email: kenterprises7@aol.com
Office phone: 301.870.7278

www.ingramcontent.com/pod-product-compliance
Lightning Source LLC
LaVergne TN
LVHW011322080426
835513LV00006B/159